BOOKS, LIBRARIES, AND RESEARCH

Mary G. Hauer
Ruth C. Murray
Doris B. Dantin
Myrtle S. Bolner

Louisiana State University
Baton Rouge, Louisiana

KENDALL/HUNT PUBLISHING COMPANY
2460 Kerper Boulevard, Dubuque, Iowa 52001

Copyright © 1979 by Kendall/Hunt Publishing Company

Library of Congress Catalog Card Number: 78-70655

ISBN 0—8403—1953—3

Printed in the United States of America

B   401953   01

To Ella V. Aldrich Schwing a pioneer in the field of library instruction for college students and author of one of the first textbooks in this field

Contents

About the cover:

The Torch of Learning forms the dominant note in the center of the sculptured metal screen located in the south lobby of the Louisiana State University Library in Baton Rouge. The whole screen is a symbolic representation of the place of man in time and is a striking example of contemporary American sculpture. It was specifically designed for its present location and forms an appropriate blending of polished metal against the modern architectural background of the LSU library. The work was designed and executed by sculptor Frank Engle.

1. Eternity
2. Universe
3. Sun
4. Stars
5. Moon
6. Challenge
7. Arts
8. Philosophy
9. Flower
10. Religion
11. Learning
12. Law and Justice
13. Sea
14. Science
15. Civilization
16. Plant Life
17. Bat
18. Earth
19. Sea Life
20. Reptile
21. Fish
22. Dividing Cell
23. Insects

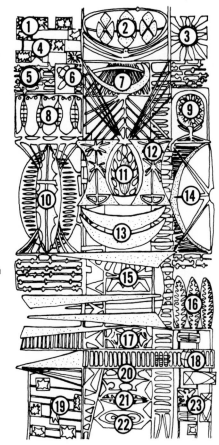

Preface

The purpose of this book is to provide a guide for students learning to use the library or for any one needing help in finding materials for a research paper. The book discusses the principal library sources—the card catalog, reference books, including the different types of indexes, and government publications. The authors have suggested titles of many reference books and indexes on a wide variety of subjects. Many of these have been annotated, while others are simply listed.

Chapter 3 gives a systematic guide to planning, researching, writing, and documenting a research paper. We have attempted to offer a number of clear models of documentation for the serious research paper, including footnotes (or endnotes) and bibliographical entries. The forms recommended are based on the *MLA Handbook for Writers of Research Papers, Theses, and Dissertations* (1977 ed.).

We wish to thank George J. Guidry, Jr., Director of the Library, the members of the Technical Services Department, the Central Reference Department, and the Government Documents Department of the Louisiana State University Library for their assistance and suggestions. Two graduate assistants, Claire McCoy and Connie Dunham, also deserve acknowledgment for their research work. Two student workers, Lindsay Bullock and Jeri Laster, are due special thanks for their tireless effort in typing the manuscript.

The authors express appreciation to the holders of copyrights for their permission to use their material.

1

INTRODUCTION TO COLLEGE AND UNIVERSITY LIBRARIES

Through the ages, man's learning about himself—his physical environment, his political and social order, his scientific and technical accomplishments, and, indeed, all aspects of his world—has been systematically collected and organized in libraries. The library has made it possible for man to preserve and locate those elements of his past which contribute to his progress. Viewed in this light, it is clear that a crucial part of one's education is to develop an appreciation for the role of libraries in our culture and, more specifically, to acquire skill in the retrieval and use of the wide-ranging resources of libraries. Since the best way to acquire this skill is through specific instruction, many colleges provide courses designed to familiarize students with the library and with research techniques. Such courses give the student an opportunity to learn skills which will make library use an integral part of his college experience. The student will find that library skills are essential to successful completion of many courses in his curriculum. Knowing beforehand how to locate information in the library can make these tasks considerably less difficult.

Most students are introduced to libraries in elementary or high school. The college or university library, however, is larger and more complex; usually it is even larger than the public library with which students are familiar. It is the mark of a good university to have a large library—one which will meet the research and instructional needs of the faculty as well as the needs of the graduate and undergraduate student. Every university library has a great number of books, magazines, newspapers, and documents, as well as material on microfilm, movie film, phonographic records, magnetic tapes, and other audio-visual materials. The amount of information being published grows daily and the university, as no other institution, has an obligation to make this information accessible to students, faculty, and others interested in research. College and university libraries in the second half of the twentieth century have had to face a two-fold problem—an enormous increase in the volume of published information and unprecedented increases in the student population. In the late seventies college enrollments have leveled off from the surge that began after World War II. The task of providing for maximum use of the library by students and faculty is also made complex by the diversity of needs within the university.

For years librarians have been studying library arrangements and services in order to meet the needs of all those whom the library serves. While there is some uniformity of arrangement among college and university libraries, there are also many variations. Differences in arrangement from library to library depend upon the function of the college or university. Some schools have separate libraries for undergraduates; other schools have only one central library; some universities have established branch libraries to serve various colleges or departments within the university. Beyond the question of locating library facilities on campus for maximum use, librarians are also concerned with arranging materials within the library.

TRADITIONAL ARRANGEMENT

Prior to the "information explosion" of the 1950's, most libraries had arrived at an arrangement generally known as the *traditional plan*. Under this arrangement books are arranged by call number in the stack area of the library. Some libraries have "closed" stacks—only library staff and those with special permission have access to the stacks. Patrons present a "call slip" to a library attendant who gets the material. In most modern libraries, however, patrons are free to browse in "open" stacks and select material from the shelves.

Reference Department

Books such as encyclopedias, dictionaries, almanacs, handbooks, and indexes which are frequently used for finding information are kept in a separate area. Reference librarians familiar with this collection are available to help patrons find information in the reference department.

Periodical Department

Periodicals are shelved together in one area for convenience of use. Some libraries have found that it is more feasible to have only the current periodicals in one area with the bound volumes of periodicals in a separate area or in the stacks with other books.

Browsing Room

One especially inviting place in the library is the browsing room. This room exhibits to patrons the full range of rich materials for sheer enjoyment and recreation. One can browse at leisure and select from the most recent books or from the classics.

Newspaper Room

Usually current newspapers are kept for a limited period of time in the newspaper room. Some libraries house newspapers and microform together since the older issues of newspapers are often preserved on microfilm.

Reserve Book Room

A necessary collection in the college and university library is the reserve book collection. Books which are needed for classes are placed together in the reserve book room in order to insure their availability for those who will be using them for assigned reading.

Listening Department

The records, cassette tapes, and other "listening" materials in the library's collection require special equipment and handling. Listening rooms are designed to facilitate the use of these materials.

Government Publications

Many university libraries serve as depositories for United States and United Nations documents. These are shelved separately in a special area. Some libraries locate state and local government documents in the documents room, but it is also quite common to house these materials in a distinct "state" room designed to preserve, in all forms, materials dealing with the particular state.

Archives

Original source material such as letters, manuscripts, diaries, personal records, and other unpublished material are an important part of the research library and are customarily placed in an archives department. Archivists staffing this department perform invaluable reference and acquisition functions.

Rare Books

University librarians, like most book collectors, pride themselves in assembling books which are valuable because of their artistic and/or unique qualities or because they are old and no longer available. Such books need protection and care in handling. They are shelved in specially designed areas and are not allowed to circulate.

Special Collections

In fulfilling its research function a university library frequently has a number of highly specialized collections. The advantage of such collections is that they support the university's effort to become a center for research in particular subject fields.

DIVISIONAL ARRANGEMENT

A somewhat different approach to library arrangement is the *divisional arrangement*. In this arrangement all the books, periodicals, pamphlets, reference tools, and reserve books in a field of knowledge are placed together in the same area. The books are in "open" stacks, with the patron free to choose his own material. Typical divisions are Humanities, Sciences, and Social Sciences. Each division has its own reference librarians and staff assistants.

Some libraries with the divisional arrangement usually have other departments such as Government Documents, Newspaper and Microfilm Room, Rare Books, Listening Room, and Archives. Some have separate rooms for reserved books; others have reserved book sections in each division.

TRENDS

Like almost every other aspect of American life, libraries have experienced their share of "future shock." The well-known information explosion has resulted in a staggering increase in publications each year; new fields of knowledge are constantly being explored. The most futuristic development in the library field, however, is represented by computer technology. Computers were first used in libraries in the technical services—circulation, serials records, cataloging, and acquisitions. Now computers are being used to perform reference services—to compile bibliographies, indexes, and catalogs. Interchange of materials among libraries has greatly accelerated as a result of improved computer technology. Some libraries are already linked by telephone to computer-based terminals which make it possible to check their holdings almost immediately. It is not far-fetched to envision libraries of the future linked together by computers which can reproduce material over long distances instantaneously. The library of the future might also include computerized consoles in place of the card catalog. Research would become a push-button operation.

Computers, as well as other scientific advances, are of increasing importance to libraries. Knowing all the facilities made possible by technology will increase the user's research capability immeasurably.

Interlibrary Loan

Most public and institutional libraries subscribe to the Interlibrary Loan Code adopted by the American Library Association in 1968. It is designed to permit libraries to cooperate in exchanging materials. The rising cost of library operations and acquisitions have forced more and more libraries to seek cooperation with other institutions in order to serve the patrons. Libraries lend each other books and other materials which are unavailable at the local library. The loans are for limited periods, and the cost of borrowing material (postage, handling, and duplication) are generally borne by the borrower.

Library Cooperatives

A practice which is prevalent among libraries today is that of forming a cooperative for the purpose of making holdings or services available to cooperative members and their patrons on a reciprocal basis. These groups are known by various names: library networks, information centers, consortia, library systems. Some groups share general printed materials while others share specialized materials such as periodicals, films, slides, and other audio-visual material.

Regional library systems are widespread across the United States. The libraries in a geographical area form the regional systems to share their holdings among members. It is expected that within a few years the regional systems will be linked to create a national library network. It will then be possible to locate any item needed for research almost immediately. The creation of such a system is well under way. The OCLC (Ohio College Library Center) began some years ago as a consortium of Ohio college libraries. OCLC went far beyond merely making its holdings available to consortium members. It devised a computerized catalog of its holdings. Members of OCLC had direct access to the computerized central catalog through computer terminals. Other libraries joined OCLC in order to have access to the computerized catalog. In 1976 the number of libraries holding membership in OCLC was 675, and the membership has continued to grow. Some libraries contract to use the computer resources of OCLC, such as its computerized cataloging service, but are not full participating members. Members of OCLC can now handle requests for interlibrary loan material. The holdings of all member institutions are listed in one computerized catalog. Requests are made by author or title. Answers are received directly from OCLC, identifying the nearest location of the requested material.

Data Banks

Data bank research is the newest and most sophisticated method of locating information. Computerized data banks store millions of citations from catalogs, indexes, books, abstracts, research summaries, reports, and conference proceedings. A number of these data banks are located throughout the country.

The search is carried out by means of a terminal located in the subscribing library. The request for bibliographic information is relayed to the data bank by telephone. The computer then searches its data bank for information from among millions of articles, reports, books, and other kinds of information. The results of the search are then printed out at the terminal. Such a comprehensive search would take an individual months to complete by hand. The computer search takes as little as five to ten minutes. In the case of long bibliographies, the search may take several hours. The charges for this service vary according to the time required to complete the search and the number of citations retrieved. A well-planned search may cost less than $50.

Microform

Libraries have made great strides in reproducing materials through the process of microphotography. It is possible to copy books, monographs, and other documents on microfiche, microcard, or microfilm. Most libraries store back issues of newspapers on microfilm. In recent years the trend has been toward an increased use of microfiche for theses, dissertations, and government documents.

The information now stored on microform has been in direct response to the information explosion. It is possible to store material on microform in a fraction of the space required to store printed matter.

2
THE BOOK

Libraries have played a leading role in the scientific advancement that has brought about so much change and progress in the world today. They serve as information centers, disseminating information for immediate use and application. In turn, the application of scientific and technological advancements to the library has enhanced its performance as an information center. Today's library no longer features simply books, newspapers, magazines, and quiet study areas. Films, microform materials, computers, and a variety of electronic devices are increasingly a part of the modern library. These new resources are definitely necessary if the library is to provide the service needed in today's world. It is easy, however, to become distracted by electronic devices and plastics and to forget that it all began with the simple book. Let us take a look at the history of the book and examine its current make-up.

The oldest books were the baked clay tablets which originated in Babylon and Nineveh about 5,000 years ago. These were used primarily for keeping records such as property records and dates of events. The baked clay was a hard, durable material which has lasted to this day. However, the clay tablets were not household possessions.

The Egyptians developed a more manageable material to use for books. They made papyrus from a reedlike plant which grew along the Nile. The papyrus formed a long paper-like sheet which was rolled up and stored upright. The writing on it was done in long columns so only a small section of it need be unrolled at a time in order to read it.

The Romans used the same roll-type book for hundreds of years. In addition to the papyrus roll, the Romans also used the skin of lambs, calves, or kids to make a type of parchment called vellum. The vellum was easier to write on than papyrus. The roll book was in general usage until about 300 A.D. when the *codex* came into existence. It was a forerunner of the modern book in that it was made up of three or four sheets of vellum folded into sections and sewn together similar to the modern book.

One of the greatest contributions to civilization was made by the Chinese about 105 A.D.—the invention of paper. A thousand years later this great invention reached Europe. Paper was used in Baghdad in about 800 A.D. and in Spain in the 1100s A.D. The use of paper became widespread in Europe in the late 1400s. The use of paper in writing coincided with the increased demand for books which accompanied the beginning of the Renaissance in the 15th and 16th centuries.

For thousands of years books were written slowly and laboriously by hand. It took months and even years for the slow process of hand-copying a book to be completed. Consequently, books were available to only a few privileged scholars. The spread of classical learning which accompanied the end of the Middle Ages and the beginning of the Renaissance increased the demand for reading material. A form of hand-printing had been developed in China about 1,000 years ago, but it is doubtful that people in the West were aware of it. The first printed books in the West were hand-printed from letters carved into wooden blocks. This was a difficult and time-consuming process and was no improvement over the hand-copying method of producing manuscripts.

The invention of a movable type printing press about 1457 revolutionized bookmaking. A German printer, Johann Gutenberg, is generally given credit for the invention that was to make a monumental contribution to the intellectual development of mankind. The Gutenberg Bible was the first book printed on movable type. About 200 copies of the Gutenberg Bible were printed, 40 or 50 of which are still in existence. It was printed on a press which was made of hand-cast letters that resembled the letters in hand-written manuscripts. What was truly innovative about Gutenberg's press was that once a book had been printed the same type could be reassembled and used again for printing other books.

Within a few years printing had spread throughout Europe, and the number of books being produced increased tremendously. By the end of the fifteenth century more than 30,000 different books had been printed. Book printing became an art form with much attention being paid to the physical beauty of the book, the artistic quality of the letters, the type of cover and paper used, and the decoration of the end papers and the edges of the book.

The simple techniques developed by Gutenberg remained unchanged until the early 1800's when improvements in papermaking made the printing process much faster. In 1884 the linotype was invented, making possible the setting of an entire line of type with one operation. For a period printers stopped concentrating on the art of book printing and emphasized instead the mechanics of the trade. It is not surprising that the outstanding result was the mass production of books.

Book publishing flourished after World War II when the paperback book came into widespread use. As demand for these less expensive copies of books has continued to increase, publishers have developed less expensive methods of printing books. *Offset* printing has now largely replaced the letterpress method of book printing. Happily, the boom in publishing has brought about a renewed interest in the artistic aspect of book printing leading to the production, once again, of fine quality books for all ages.

PARTS OF THE BOOK

If we were to define a book, we would say that it consists of leaves of paper fastened together at one edge and covered with a protective cover. The first printed books lacked a title and introductory pages. A colophon at the end of the text described the type used and frequently included the printer's distinctive mark. Publishers have developed a uniformity in the arrangement of the contents of the book which enhances its usability.

Book Cover

The cover of the book, of course, holds the pages of the book together and protects them. The edge of the cover where the pages are bound together is called the spine. On the spine are ordinarily printed the short-title of the book, the author's name, the publisher, and, in the case of library books, the call number. The front of the cover is usually decorated. It may also give the author's name and the short-title of the book. The end papers are those sheets attached to the inside of the front and back covers.

Preliminary Pages

There are several pages which precede the text of the book and give the reader some idea of what it contains. These preliminary pages are usually numbered with small Roman numerals. They include the following:

1. The *flyleaves* are blank pages next to the end papers.
2. The *half-title* page gives the short-title of the book and the name of the series if the book is one of a series.
3. The *frontispiece* is an illustration or portrait which faces the title page.
4. The *title page* is the first significant page in the book. It is always on the right, or *recto,* of the leaf. The left side of a leaf is known as the *verso.* The following information can be found on the title page:

   Title. The full name of the book, including the *subtitle* or *descriptive title.*

   Author. The author's name and usually a list of credentials such as degrees, academic position, and, occasionally, the names of other works.

   Editor, Compiler, Illustrator, or *Translator.* Anyone other than the author who has made a significant contribution to the book.

   Edition. Given if the book is other than a first edition. All copies of a book printed from one set of type make up an edition. *Reprints* are copies of the same edition printed at a later time. When any changes are made, it is a *revised edition* or a new edition.

   Imprint. The place of publication, the publisher, and the date of publication at the bottom of the title page. The publication date is sometimes omitted from the title page.

5. The *verso* of the title page gives the copyright notice and the printing history of the book. The copyright guarantees ownership of a book and protects the owner's rights. When a *copyright* is secured, two copies of the book are placed in the Library of Congress. Recently, it has become the practice to print a copy of the catalog card on the verso of the title page.
6. The *dedication* page gives a brief announcement in which the author dedicates the book to another person or persons.
7. The *preface* or *foreword* gives the author's purpose in writing the book and acknowledges those persons who have helped in its preparation.
8. The *table of contents* lists in order the chapters or parts of the book and gives the pages on which they are located. Some books include a brief summary of each chapter in the table of contents.
9. The *list of illustrations* gives the pages on which illustrative material can be found.
10. The *introduction* describes the subject and gives a preliminary statement leading into the main contents of the book.

Text and Notes

The main body of printed matter is the text of the book. It is usually divided into chapters or separate parts and includes explanatory material and identification of reference sources in the form of *footnotes* at the bottom of the page. Some books have *notes* at the end of chapters, others at the end of the book.

Auxiliary Material

Auxiliary or reference materials at the end of the book aid the readers using the book. These may include:

1. *Glossary.* A list with definitions of the technical terms or unusual words used in the text.
2. *Appendix.* Supplementary materials such as tables or maps.
3. *Notes.* If they are not included with the text, they are placed at the end of the book.
4. *Bibliography.* A list of all books, articles, and other material the author used in writing the book. It may also include other materials which are relevant to the subject.
5. *Index.* An alphabetical list of the subjects discussed in the book, along with the corresponding page numbers.

Some books may not have all the different parts described in this chapter, and sometimes the order of their appearance may vary.

3
THE RESEARCH PAPER

Generally speaking, the student's educational career is characterized by two kinds of learning: (1) passive learning, involving exposure to "facts" with an emphasis on memorization and (2) active learning in which the student inquires into questions which have stirred his interest and curiosity. The student's college or university career—if it is to be rewarding—must be marked by active learning. It is anticipated that the student will learn much more than "spoon-fed" facts. At a minimum, the undergraduate student is expected to prepare himself for living by learning how to locate and use information. The graduate student is expected to prepare himself to become a participant in the creation of new knowledge. Teachers seeking to develop their students' skills will usually rely on some type of formal writing. The most common type of writing exercise is the term paper, usually a formal essay requiring library research. The term paper offers the student an opportunity to examine issues, locate material relevant to an issue, digest, analyze, and present the information with his conclusions and interpretations.

Before undertaking a research project, the student should have some knowledge of library resources. The remaining chapters of this book are designed to guide the student through the library. Bewilderment at having to write a research paper should be considerably lessened by knowing something about the library's organization and how its resources can be used effectively. It is also helpful to approach the term paper assignment as a series of stages or steps rather than as a single, perhaps overwhelming, task. Seven rather obvious steps are: (1) selecting a topic, (2) formulating a thesis, (3) preparing an outline, (4) gathering information and taking notes, (5) writing the text of the paper, (6) preparing the footnotes or endnotes and bibliography, and (7) typing the final draft. Let us examine each of these steps in some detail.

SELECTING A TOPIC

Sometimes the initial step in the preparation of a research paper is the most challenging one. The selection of a topic is also the most crucial one in determining the success of the research paper. If the instructor assigns a topic, the student need only determine how he will proceed. In most cases, however, the student must choose his own topic.

There are several overriding principles to consider in choosing a research topic. The first one is to select a topic that is interesting, that will arouse the researcher's curiosity and stir his imagination. Although research means examining and using the ideas of others, the researcher must also project his own thought and creativity. For this reason, it is important to select a topic that is not completely new. If the student knows nothing about the topic, probably he will not be predisposed to investigate it, and the research process might prove tedious and boring.

Second, the topic should be appropriate for the length of the paper which has been assigned. A study on "Civil Rights" would be much too broad for a ten-page research paper.

"Civil Rights of American Indians Living on Indian Reservations" would be more suitable. In order to narrow an overly broad subject, the student should conduct a preliminary library search. A general encyclopedia is a good source to consult in this initial step. Although the encyclopedia gives a broad overview of a topic, it also provides ideas for the subject's narrower aspects. In the article on the Supreme Court of the United States in *Encyclopaedia Britannica,* one can find references to the court's historical development, its procedures, and landmark decisions. From the article the reader should be able to find one specific aspect of the court worthy of further investigation and narrow enough to cover in ten pages.

Third, one should consider the availability of research materials. Again, a general encyclopedia might serve as a guide. The bibliography provided at the end of the article indicates the availability of research materials. A quick search in the card catalog or in a periodical index will also help.

FORMULATING A THESIS

After the student has familiarized himself somewhat with the topic selected, the second step is to determine the *purpose* of the paper. What will be the focus? What is to be proven or shown in the paper? The thesis statement should be concise and precise, stating in as few words as possible the paper's purpose and the approach to be used.

PREPARING THE OUTLINE

The third step is to prepare a working outline that includes all the facets of the topic to be investigated. To be useful the outline should divide the paper's contents into a number of major parts; each of these parts should be further divided and subdivided until the student can visualize the outline as a guide for research and as the skeleton for the final report. A sample outline is shown below.

EXAMPLE OF TOPIC OUTLINE

Topic: U.S. Conversion to the Metric System

Thesis: This paper will examine the characteristics and uses of the metric system and the inevitable conversion process that faces all Americans.

Outline:

  I. History of systems of weights and measures
     A. Ancient
     B. British
     C. Other systems of weights and measures

 II. Metric system of weights and measures
     A. Development and use
     B. Units of measurement
     C. Advantages and disadvantages

III. Weights and measures in the U.S.
    A. History
    B. Present-day status in relation to other countries
    C. The "Great Metric Controversy"
        1. Arguments for conversion
            a. Economic
            b. Conformity
            c. Ease of use
        2. Arguments against conversion
            a. Cost of conversion
            b. Effect on U.S. citizens and U.S. industry
            c. Satisfaction with customary system
    D. Congressional action
        1. Metric Conversion Act
        2. National Metric Conversion Board
    E. How conversion would take place
        1. Cost
        2. Educating the public
        3. Time allowed for conversion

GATHERING INFORMATION AND TAKING NOTES

Armed with the outline the student is now ready for step number four—gathering information. It is assumed that the student is familiar with the library's facilities. He must know how to locate the appropriate library materials dealing with his topic. The major sources to consult in the library search are: (1) the card catalog, (2) reference books, (3) indexes, (4) government documents, and (5) the vertical file.

A convenient way for the student to record what he finds is to use index cards. At the top of the card he should write the author of the work, title of the work, the edition, the place of publication, publisher, date of publication, volume number, and inclusive pages if the reference is to an article. The call number should be placed in a lower corner of the card. The forms for bibliographical entries are given on pages 17-25. It is helpful to know the proper bibliographical form before undertaking the actual research so that the necessary details need be copied only once.

After all pertinent material has been gathered by the student, he must read and carefully extract the information important for his research. Notes should be written on the index cards following each bibliographical entry. The notes may either quote the authority or summarize what he has said. In either case it is important to retain the original meaning. Since material used out of context can be manipulated to distort the author's intended meaning, it is important to use the material to convey the author's intent. If statements are quoted directly, they should be copied exactly as they appear in the original and placed within quotation marks. Paraphrasing is the summarization of material so that the original author's meaning is retained, but rephrased by the researcher. In both cases the page or pages should be correctly noted on the note card.

WRITING THE PAPER

When the judicious researcher is satisfied that he has gathered sufficient information to support all the topics in the original outline, he is ready to begin writing the first draft of the paper. The notes should be sorted so that they are grouped under headings to fit the topics in the outline. In making the first draft of the paper, the student should put into practice all that he has learned about writing in the past—effective phrasing of ideas, good paragraph development, and attention to logical flow of the paragraphs into a unified paper.

The research paper, by definition, is based primarily on evidence gathered from authorities and scholars. It demands a great deal of creativity to assimilate evidence and present it so that it gives the reader a new perspective. Sufficient time should be allowed for the actual writing. It may take several drafts to achieve the well-written research paper.

Plagiarism

The appropriation of ideas or the copying of the language of another writer without formal acknowledgment is *plagiarism*. Plagiarism is a serious violation of legal and ethical canons; yet many students who would not dare copy another's examination paper think nothing of "borrowing" ideas and even exact language from another writer without giving credit. This is not to say that the student must document every single thing he has written down. Those ideas which evolve in his own mind, even though they are a result of his research, do not require documentation. Nor is it necessary to document facts considered common knowledge. Ordinarily the student should not have difficulty determining what is common knowledge. He should notice in his readings that well-known facts, such as the date of America's entry into World War I, require no documentation. Little known facts, or facts of which the student has no prior knowledge, such as details of President Wilson's peace proposals, would require documentation. If there is doubt in the student's mind as to whether or not a fact is common knowledge, he should acknowledge his source.

FOOTNOTES OR ENDNOTES

The accepted form used to document a source is the footnote (appearing at the bottom of the page) or endnotes (appearing at the end of the paper). Occasionally the instructor will indicate a preference for the location of notes in a research paper. In the text of the paper, documented material is indicated by a "superscript" (a raised Arabic number) placed behind the punctuation mark of material that is quoted or paraphrased. The note numbers should be consecutive throughout the paper.

Arrangement and Punctuation

The first line of the note (footnote or endnote) is indented five spaces to the right. It begins with the raised number ("superscript") followed by the author's name or first word in the title. The second line of the note begins at the left margin. The author's name is given in regular order (first name, middle name or initial, and last name). Words in the title are capitalized, except articles, prepositions, and conjunctions unless one is the first word in a title. Each word in the title is underlined. A comma follows the author's name, the title, the editor, the edition, and the series unless one of these is followed immediately by parenthesis. The facts of publication (city, publisher, date) are enclosed in parentheses. A colon follows the name of the city, and a comma follows the publisher's name. A comma is placed after the parenthesis mark and before the page number. The page number refers to the specific citation.

Subsequent references to the same work are cited in shortened form.

Example:

Book

    [15]Barbara Tuchman, <u>The Guns of August</u> (New York: Macmillan, 1962), p. 133.
    [16]Tuchman, p. 186.

Periodical Article

    [22]Jeannette F. Tudor, "Development of Class Awareness in Children," <u>Social Forces</u>, 49 (1971), 473.
    [23]Tudor, p. 479.

Formerly, "ibid." (meaning "in the same place") was used for two or more references in sequence. Current usage is to identify the work being cited with the relevant page numbers. In most cases the author's last name is sufficient to identify the work.

If two or more different titles by the same author are being cited, the citation should include a shortened form of the title after the author's last name. References to Henry James' *Portrait of a Lady* and his *Wings of the Dove* would be cited in subsequent references as follows:

    [25]James, <u>Wings</u>, p. 135.
    [26]James, <u>Portrait</u>, p. 202.

The terms "op. cit." ("in the work cited") and "loc. cit." ("in the place cited") are no longer considered good form.

If a single work is referred to extensively in the paper it should be identified in the first full note. Subsequent references should be included within parentheses in the text instead of in the notes.

Notes:

    [1]Walker Percy, <u>Lancelot</u> (New York: Farrar, Strauss, Giroux, c1977), p. 1. All further references to this work appear in the text.

Text:

    "In New Orleans I have noticed that people are happiest when they are going to funerals, making money, taking care of the dead, or putting on masks at Mardi Gras so nobody knows who they are" (p. 10).

If a frequently cited work can be identified easily with abbreviations, it should be cited in full in the first citation with the abbreviations given.

Notes:

⁵Samuel Eliot Morison, <u>The Oxford History of the American People</u> (New York: Oxford University Press, 1965), p. 547; hereafter cited as <u>OHAP</u>.

²⁸<u>OHAP</u>, p. 86.

THE BIBLIOGRAPHY

A bibliography is a descriptive list of sources of information—books, articles from periodicals, government documents, theses and dissertations, articles from reference books, and other sources of information. A bibliography may list works by one author (an *author* bibliography), or it may list references on a subject (a *subject* bibliography). A *selective* bibliography includes only some of the possible references, while a *complete* bibliography lists all the references available. Bibliographies with descriptive notes about each entry are called *annotated* bibliographies.

A bibliography for a research paper includes all the sources of information used in writing the paper. It is placed at the end of the paper following the endnotes. Items in a bibliography may be grouped according to their form of publication. For example, books may be listed in one group and periodicals in a second group. Within each group, the items are arranged in alphabetical order according to author surnames or, in cases where no author is given, according to the first word of the title excluding "a," "an," and "the."

Arrangement and Punctuation

Books in the bibliography are arranged alphabetically according to the last name of the author. If there is more than one author, only the first name listed is inverted. If the book is listed by title rather than author, it is placed alphabetically by words in the title. If two or more entries have the same author, the author's name is not repeated. A seven space line is used to indicate the omission of the name. The first line of each entry is placed in *hanging indention*. That is, it begins about four spaces to the left of the following lines in the entry.

A period is placed after the author's name, another after the title, and another after each separate item except after the items in the *imprint* (publication information). A colon follows the place of publication; a comma comes between the publisher and the date. A period is placed at the end of the entry.

GENERAL RULES—NOTES AND BIBLIOGRAPHY

To prepare footnotes or endnotes and bibliographies properly, one needs to know certain elementary forms of documentation. While there is no one "correct" form for documentation, convention does dictate that the writer of scholarly papers follow a prescribed style—one that is consistent throughout and which communicates clearly and accurately the sources which are being documented. The form for notes and bibliography discussed below is based on *The MLA Style Sheet,* which is widely used throughout the United States. For a more exhaustive treatment, one should consult the *MLA Handbook for Writers of Research Papers, Theses, and Dissertations* (New York: Modern Language Association, 1977).

Note style and bibliography style vary only in arrangement and punctuation. The items included in each entry are essentially the same with the exception of the page reference which is omitted in a bibliographical entry for a book.

I. BOOKS

Items to include in documenting a book:

1. Author's full name.
2. The title of the book, as it appears on the title page.
3. Editor, translator, illustrator, compiler (if any).
4. The edition if other than the first.
5. The series (if any). Series titles are neither underlined nor placed within quotation marks.
6. Total number of volumes if a multivolume set.
7. The city of publication. If more than one place is listed on the title page, only the first one listed is used. The name of the state is included if the city is not well-known.
8. The publisher. The shortened name of the publisher is used unless there is confusion in identification.
9. The date of publication. Publication date is found on the title page. If there is no publication date given, the latest copyright date is used. If neither publication nor copyright date is given, the abbreviation, n.d., is used.
10. Page citation for a note entry.

Examples:

A. Books by one author

Notes:

     ¹Ethel Hausman, <u>The Illustrated Encyclopedia of American Wildflowers</u>, il. Tabea Hofmann and the author (Garden City, N.Y.: Garden City Publishing Co., 1947), p. 28.

Bibliography:

Hausman, Ethel. <u>The Illustrated Encyclopedia of American Wildflowers</u>. Il. Tabea Hofmann and the author. Garden City, N.Y.: Garden City Publishing Co., 1947.

(The illustrator is included since this information is found on the title page. The state in which the book was published is given because the city is not a familiar one. The publisher's full name is given here to avoid confusion with the name of the city.)

B. Books by two or three authors

Notes:

     ²Wallace K. Ferguson and Geoffrey Bruum, <u>A Survey of European Civilization</u>, 2nd ed. (Boston: Houghton Mifflin, 1952), p. 73.

Bibliography:

Ferguson, Wallace K., and Geoffrey Bruum. <u>A Survey of European Civilization</u>. 2nd ed. Boston: Houghton Mifflin, 1952.

(The name of the first author is inverted in the bibliographical entry. Names of other authors are given in regular order. These are given in the order in which they appear on the title page.)

C.   Books by more than three persons

Notes:

[3]James Davis, et al., <u>Society and the Law: New Meanings for an Old Profession</u> (New York: Free Press of Glencoe, c1962), p. 102.

Bibliography:

Davis, James, et al. <u>Society and the Law: New Meanings for an Old Profession</u>. New York: Free Press of Glencoe, c1962.

(or: Davis, James, and others)

D.   Corporate author

Notes:

[4]Center for the Study of Democratic Institutions, <u>Natural Law and Modern Society</u>, contrib. John Cogley, et al. (Cleveland: World, 1973), p. 157.

Bibliography:

Center for the Study of Democratic Institutions. <u>Natural Law and Modern Society</u>. Contrib. John Cogley, et al. Cleveland: World, 1973.

E.   A collection of different authors' works, edited by different persons

Notes:

[5]Phillip Green and Michael Walzer, eds., <u>The Political Imagination in Literature: A Reader</u> (New York: Free Press, c1969), p. 28.

Bibliography:

Green, Phillip, and Michael Walzer, eds. <u>The Political Imagination in Literature: A Reader</u>. New York: Free Press, c1969.

F.   A volume in a series

Notes:

[6]Lacy H. Hunt, <u>Dynamics of Forecasting Financial Cycles: Theory, Technique, and Implementation</u>, foreword Robert A. Kavesh, Contemporary Studies in Economic and Financial Analysis, vol. 1 (Greenwich, Conn.: JAI Press, c1976), p. 18.

Bibliography:

Hunt, Lacy H. <u>Dynamics of Forecasting Financial Cycles: Theory, Technique, and Implementation</u>. Foreword Robert A. Kavesh. Contemporary Studies in Economic and Financial Analysis, vol. 1. Greenwich, Conn.: JAI Press, c1976.

G. Books in a multivolume work, one author, each volume a different title

Notes:

[7]Dumas Malone, <u>Jefferson and the Ordeal of Liberty</u>, Vol. III of <u>Jefferson and His Time</u> (Boston: Little, Brown, 1962), p. 243.

Bibliography:

Malone, Dumas. <u>Jefferson and the Ordeal of Liberty</u>. Vol. III of <u>Jefferson and His Time</u>. Boston: Little, Brown, 1962.

H. Multivolume work with one general title

Notes:

[8]Henry Adams, <u>The Education of Henry Adams: An Introduction</u>, introd. Marion L. Starkey, Time Reading Program Special Edition, 2 vols. (New York: Time, 1964).

(If citing the entire multivolume work)

[9]Charles Warren, <u>The Supreme Court in United States History</u>, rev. ed. (Boston: Little, Brown, c1926), I, 231.

(If citing one volume of a multivolume work)

Bibliography:

Adams, Henry. <u>The Education of Henry Adams: An Introduction</u>. Introd. Marion L. Starkey. Time Reading Program Special Edition. 2 vols. New York: Time, 1964.
Warren, Charles. <u>The Supreme Court in United States History</u>. Rev. ed. Vol. I. Boston: Little, Brown, c1926.

I. A translation of an author's work

Notes:

[10]Friedrich Nietzsche, <u>The Birth of Tragedy and the Genealogy of Morals</u>, trans. Francis Golffing (Garden City, N.Y.: Doubleday, 1956), p. 42.

Bibliography:

Nietzsche, Friedrich. <u>The Birth of Tragedy and the Genealogy of Morals</u>. Trans. Francis Golffing. Garden City, N.Y.: Doubleday, 1956.

J.   A short story in a collected work (anthology)

Notes:

[11]William Faulkner, "Dry September," in <u>Ten Modern Masters: An Anthology of the Short Story</u>, ed. Robert G. Davis (New York: Harcourt, Brace, c1953), p. 340.

Bibliography:

Faulkner, William. "Dry September." In <u>Ten Modern Masters: An Anthology of the Short Story</u>. Ed. Robert G. Davis. New York: Harcourt, Brace, c1953, p. 340.

K.   An essay in a collected work (anthology)

Notes:

[12]James D. Barker, "Man, Mood, and the Presidency," in <u>The Presidency Reappraised</u>, ed. Rexford G. Tugwell and Thomas E. Cronin (New York: Praeger, c1974), p. 208.

Bibliography:

Barker, James D. "Man, Mood, and the Presidency." In <u>The Presidency Reappraised</u>. Ed. Rexford G. Tugwell and Thomas E. Cronin. New York: Praeger, c1974, pp. 205-214.

II.   REFERENCE BOOKS

In citing articles from general encyclopedias, yearbooks, biographical dictionaries, and other well-known reference books, the following items are included:

1.   The author of the article, if known.
2.   The title of the article as it appears in the book.
3.   The title of the book in which the article appears.
4.   The edition, if other than the first, or the date of publication, or the copyright date.
5.   The volume number if one of a multivolume set.
6.   The inclusive paging for a bibliographical entry; specific page for a note entry.

Examples:

A.   An article from a multi-volume reference book

Notes:

[13]Leroy D. Vandam, "Anesthetic," <u>The New Encyclopaedia Britannica: Macropaedia</u> (c1974), I, 886.

Bibliography:

Vandam, Leroy D. "Anesthetic." <u>The New Encyclopaedia Britannica: Macropaedia</u>, c1974, I, 886-889.

B.   An article from a single volume reference book

Notes:

[14]Romulo Betancourt, "Latin America, Its Problems and Possibilities," Britannica Book of the Year, 1966 (c1966), p. 26.

Bibliography:

Betancourt, Romulo. "Latin America, Its Problems and Possibilities." Britannica Book of the Year, 1966, c1966, pp. 19-40.

C.   An article from a biographical dictionary

Notes:

[15]"Sellers, Peter (Richard Henry)," Who's Who 1976-1977 (c1976), p. 2139.

Bibliography:

"Sellers, Peter (Richard Henry)." Who's Who 1976-1977, c1976, pp. 2139-2140.

Notes:

[16]Arthur C. Cole, "Webster, Daniel," Dictionary of American Biography (c1936), XIX , 587.

Bibliography:

Cole, Arthur C. "Webster, Daniel." Dictionary of American Biography, c1936, XIX, 585-592.

D.   A book of quotations

Notes:

[17]Samuel Johnson, "He who praises everybody praises nobody. . .," The Oxford Dictionary of Quotations, 2nd ed., p. 237.

Bibliography:

Johnson, Samuel. "He who praises everybody praises nobody. . . ." The Oxford Dictionary of Quotations, 2nd ed., p. 237.

E.   An article from a multivolume subject reference book

Notes:

[18]Eleanor Flexner, "Woman's Rights Movement," Dictionary of American History, ed. J.G.E. Hopkins and Wayne Andrews (New York: Scribner, 1961), VI (Supp. 1), 301.

Bibliography:

Flexner, Eleanor. "Woman's Rights Movement." <u>Dictionary of American History</u>. Ed. J.G.E. Hopkins and Wayne Andrews. New York: Scribner, 1961. VI (Supp. 1), 301–303.

(If the reference book is not a familiar one or if there are other books with the same title, it is necessary to give full publication information.)

III. MAGAZINE AND NEWSPAPER ARTICLES

In citing articles from periodicals the following items are included:
1. The author of the article if it is a signed article.
2. The title of the article.
3. The title of the periodical.
4. The volume number and issue number if it is a journal.
5. The date.
6. The inclusive pages in a bibliographical entry; the specific page reference in a note entry.

Examples:

A.   A signed article from a monthly magazine

Notes:

  [19]Roger Starr, "A Kind Word about Money," <u>Harper's</u>, April 1976, p. 90.

Bibliography:

Starr, Roger. "A Kind Word about Money." <u>Harper's</u>, April 1976, pp. 79-92.
(For a monthly magazine only the date and pages, not the volume, are cited.)

B.   An unsigned article from a monthly magazine

Notes:

  [20]"First National Data on Reading Speed," <u>Intellect</u>, October 1972, p. 9.

Bibliography:

"First National Data on Reading Speed." <u>Intellect</u>, October 1972, p. 9.

C.   An unsigned article from a weekly magazine

Notes:

  [21]"Behind the Threat of More Inflation," <u>Business Week</u>, 18 Nov. 1972, p. 77.

Bibliography:

"Behind the Threat of More Inflation." <u>Business Week</u>, 18 Nov. 1972, pp. 76-78.

D.   An article from a journal in which pages are numbered continuously throughout the year

Notes:

[22]Gerald Runkle, "Is Violence Always Wrong?" Journal of Politics, 38 (1976), 250.

Bibliography:

Runkle, Gerald. "Is Violence Always Wrong?" Journal of Politics, 38 (1976), 247-291.
(The volume number, the year, and the pages are cited. The abbreviations for volume and page are not used when a volume number and a page number are both cited in an entry.)

E.   An article from a journal in which pages of each issue are numbered separately

Notes:

[23]Jay Martin, "A Watertight Watergate Future: Americans in a Post-American Age," The Antioch Review, 33, No. 2 (1975), 18.

Bibliography:

Martin, Jay. "A Watertight Watergate Future: Americans in a Post-American Age." The Antioch Review, 33, No. 2 (1975), 7-25.
(Volume number, issue number, year, and pages are cited.)

F.   A signed book review

Notes:

[24]Robert Sherrill, rev. of The Time of Illusion, by Jonathan Schell, New York Times Book Review, 18 Jan. 1976, p. 1.

Bibliography:

Sherrill, Robert. Rev. of The Time of Illusion, by Jonathan Schell. New York Times Book Review, 18 Jan. 1976, pp. 1-2.

G.   A signed book review with a title

Notes:

[25]Robert Hughes, "The Sorcerer's Apprentice," rev. of Journey to Ixtlan, by Carlos Castaneda, Time, 6 Nov. 1972, p. 101.

Bibliography:

Hughes, Robert. "The Sorcerer's Apprentice." Rev. of Journey to Ixtlan, by Carlos Castaneda. Time, 6 Nov. 1972, p. 101.

H.   An unsigned review

Notes:

[26]Rev. of The Efficacy of Law, by Harry W. Jones, Choice, September 1970, p. 941.

Bibliography:
Rev. of The Efficacy of Law, by Harry W. Jones. Choice, September 1970, p. 941.

I.   A signed newspaper article

Notes:
[27]Tom Goldstein, "New Federal Tax Law Could Foster Growth of Plans to Provide Prepaid Legal Services," New York Times, 28 Sept. 1976, p. 36, col. 3.

Bibliography:
Goldstein, Tom. "New Federal Tax Law Could Foster Growth of Plans to Provide Prepaid Legal Services." New York Times, 28 Sept. 1976, p. 36, cols. 3-5.

J.   Unsigned newspaper article

Notes:
[28]"College Enrollment Decline Predicted for South in '80's," Morning Advocate (Baton Rouge), 28 Sept. 1976, sec. B, p 7, col. 4.

Bibliography:
"College Enrollment Decline Predicted for South in '80's." Morning Advocate (Baton Rouge), 28 Sept. 1976, sec. B, p. 7, cols. 4-5.

IV. UNPUBLISHED THESIS

Notes:
[29]Carol A. Runnels, "The Self Image of the Artist . . . ," Thesis Louisiana State University, 1975, p. 10.

Bibliography:
Runnels, Carol A. "The Self Image of the Artist. . . ." Thesis Louisiana State University, 1975.

V. PHONOGRAPH RECORDINGS

Notes:
[30]Elise Bell, The Bronze Bow, based on the book by Elizabeth George Speare, Newbery Award Records, NAR 3029, 1972.

Bibliography:
Bell, Elise. The Bronze Bow. Based on the book by Elizabeth George Speare. Newbery Award Records, NAR 3029, 1972.

VI. MUSICAL SCORE

Notes:
[31]Kelly Bryan, March—Washington D.C. (London: Novello, 1971).

Bibliography:
Bryan, Kelly. <u>March—Washington D.C</u>. London: Novello, 1971.

ABBREVIATIONS

anon.	anonymous
bibliog.	bibliography
bibliog. f.	bibliographical footnote
bull.	bulletin
cf.	compare
col., cols.	column(s)
comp.	compiler, compiled by
c	copyright
ed., eds.	editor(s), edition(s), edited by
e.g.	for example
enl.	enlarged
et al.	and others
f., ff.	and following
facsim. (or facs.)	facsimile
ibid.	in the same place
il. or illus.	illustrated (by), illustrator, illustration(s)
introd.	introduction
loc. cit.	in the place cited
n. d.	no date
n. p.	no place of publication, no publisher
n. pag.	no pagination
op. cit.	in the work cited
p.	page
pp.	pages
por., pors.	portrait, portraits
pref.	preface
pseud.	pseudonym
q. v.	which see
rev.	revised (by), revision, review, reviewed (by) Review should be spelled out if any confusion arises.
[sic]	thus, so
tr., or trans.	translator, translation, translated (by)
vol., vols.	volume(s)

EXAMPLE OF AN ANNOTATED BIBLIOGRAPHY
U.S. Conversion to the Metric System
A Bibliography

Books

Branscomb, Lewis M. "Will the U.S. Go Metric?" 1973 Britannica Yearbook of Science and the Future, c1972, pp. 145-157.

      This article points out that the U.S. is one of the few countries which has not converted to the metric system. It discusses past attempts by the U.S. to convert and the gradual acceptance of metrics by other countries of the world. The author presents the arguments for conversion and tells how a ten-year conversion program would work. He traces the origin of the present system. Includes colorful metric illustrations and a table of equivalents.

Deming, Richard. Metric Power; Why and How We Are Going Metric. Nashville: T. Nelson, c1974.

      A timely book in which the author states that for the U.S. and its use of metrics, "it's all over but the shouting." It covers the history of the present system. Gives advantages of the metric system and shows how metrics will affect business and industry as well as the individual. It includes conversion tables and bibliographic references.

Donovan, Frank. Prepare Now for a Metric Future. New York: Weybright and Tally, c1970.

      An especially valuable work, this book gives the worldwide history of the use of the metric system. It compares the two systems, discusses the "Great Metric Controversy," and shows the progress of the U.S. in converting to metrics. Answers the questions "when, how, and how much?" to convert. Tables of equivalents and conversions are included.

Gilbert, Thomas F., and Marilyn B. Gilbert. Thinking Metric. New York: Wiley, c1973.

      Written for everyone facing the problem of learning a new system of weights and measures, this book includes many problems and exercises that give practice in thinking metric. It discusses the reasons the U.S. and Canada are going metric. Examines problems associated with metric units and prefixes, distance and speed, volume, weight and mass, temperature, work, power, and other quantities. There are self-tests, conversion tables, and bibliographic references.

Groner, Alex, and George A. W. Boehm. Going Metric; an AMA Survey Report. New York: AMACOM, c1973.

      A study of the results of a survey by the American Management Association of 5,500 U.S. businessmen. The research was done by questionnaire and personal interviews with businessmen, government officials, and representatives of countries that have "gone metric." It gives highlights and conclusions of the survey. There is a discussion of how U.S. businessmen feel about metrication and how the road to metrics can be made smooth. It has conversion charts, metric prefixes, and estimated cost tables.

"Metric." <u>Mathematics Dictionary</u>. Ed. Glenn James and Robert C. James. 4th ed. New York: Reinhold, 1977, pp. 248-249.

      Brief definitions of "metric density," "metric space," and "metric system." Tells of the origin of the metric system in France around 1800 and claims that it is in general use everywhere except in the English-speaking countries. Gives the basic units of measurement of the system.

National Bureau of Standards. <u>A Metric America: A Decision Whose Time Has Come</u>, by Daniel V. De Simone. Washington, D.C.: GPO, 1971.

      This work traces the history of measurement in the U.S. Arguments for going metric are based on investigations involving public hearings and surveys of groups to be affected. The impact of the changeover and future implications are discussed. Describes the ways in which other countries carried through with the conversion and the lessons learned from their experiences. Many pictures, several charts and tables, and a summary of the history of the U.S. Metric Study are included.

Williams, Dudley. "Metric System." <u>McGraw-Hill Encyclopedia of Science and Technology</u>, c1977, VIII, 404-405.

      This article discusses the development of the metric system of measurement and its spread throughout the world. Gives an explanation of its basic units along with the advantages it offers as a common basis for scientific measurement and ease of use. References are given for further reading.

Periodicals

Braithwaite, J. K. "The Effect of Metrication on Process Instrumentation." <u>Australian Journal of Instrumentation and Control</u>, 28, No. 6 (1972), 139-143.

      Along with the conversion to SI, industrial instrumentation will benefit from the rationalization of units and the avoidance of those units peculiar to certain industries and processes. Areas that could be converted include the measurements of temperature, pressure, energy, and viscosity. Another advantage to conversion is the standardization of strip charts for recorders.

"Metric System: Liters Are Coming." <u>The New York Times</u>, 27 Dec. 1974, p. 51, col. 6.

      This article discusses plans of the Seven-Up Bottling Company to replace its sixteen ounce bottle with a half-liter bottle and its quart bottle with a one-liter bottle. This will bring the company in line with the "universal trend to metric." The article points out that 90 percent of the world's population uses the metric system and predicts that Congress will take action to bring the U.S. in line with the rest of the world. Other examples of the move toward metrics in education, in the grocery stores, on the highways, etc. are given.

Parker, Frances J. "Think Metric: It's Simple." <u>American Vocational Journal</u>, 48, No. 6 (1973), 35-37.

      Written by the chairperson of the Home Economics Department at Western Michigan University, this article presents the arguments for conversion in clear and simple language. Parker discusses what the future holds for Americans concerning measurement. She argues that (1) the metric system is much simpler to use and more uniform than the 80 separate standards now in use in the U.S., (2) U.S. foreign trade necessitates conversion, (3) the U.S. is already using metrics in many ways, and (4) conversion would offer many advantages to consumers. Conversion charts and a bibliography for further reading are included.

"Still Unofficial, but—the Metric System Is Creeping in on U.S." <u>U.S. News and World Report</u>, 3 March 1975, p. 54.

      Brief description of the changes taking place in businesses, education, and federal agencies in preparing for metrication. Manufacturers such as General Motors, Caterpillar Tractor, John Deere, International Harvester, and IBM have been using metric parts for foreign trade for years and are now planning a complete changeover. Clothing manufacturers are studying the impact that buying clothing and textiles in centimeters and meters will have. Already many canned and packaged foods are carrying metric equivalents and soon will carry only metric measurements. Some states are requiring that metrics be taught in school. Weather reports giving temperature in the two systems and highway signs showing kilometers and miles are being tested. Includes a discussion of Congressional action relative to conversion.

4
CLASSIFICATION

Ever since there has been any kind of written record, attempts have been made to classify materials in some fashion. The purpose of any classification system is to bring together comparable materials so that they can be found easily and so that the library will have some logical arrangement. Early libraries sometimes arranged materials by author, color, or even size. The Library of Congress was originally arranged by size, but this became impractical when the Library began to grow very rapidly.

In most American colleges and universities either the Dewey Decimal Classification system or the Library of Congress Classification system is used. Some older universities such as Harvard University use their own system, or they have combined their system with either Dewey Decimal or Library of Congress. Other universities such as Massachusetts Institute of Technology use both systems. MIT began with the Dewey Decimal system, and when it proved inadequate, the change was made to Library of Congress. Nothing was reclassified so that books acquired before 1963 are classified in the Dewey Decimal system; materials acquired after that date are classified in the Library of Congress system. Some libraries such as Louisiana State University have reclassified or are reclassifying their entire collection into the Library of Congress system.

Ideally, books are written on one particular subject and can be classified easily under that subject. As a practical matter this is not always the case. Most books cover more than one subject. Books are classified under the largest subject covered or under what the cataloger feels is the most important subject for that library. Other subjects covered in the book are brought out by means of subject headings. For example, the book noted on page 44 *Dynamics of Forecasting Financial Cycles: Theory, Technique, and Implementation* by Lacy H. Hunt is classified under the number HG. This is the Library of Congress classification number for private finance
                     181
in the United States, but the subject headings on the catalog card indicate that the book is also about *economic forecasting* and *business cycles*.

DEWEY DECIMAL CLASSIFICATION SYSTEM

The Dewey Decimal Classification system was devised by Melvil Dewey in the latter part of the 19th century. His was not the first classification system but was one of the first based on the decimal system. The system, usually referred to as Dewey or DC, divides all knowledge into 10 different classes. These 10 primary classes are further sub-divided by several sets of subclasses. Within the subclasses, the cataloger is able to show even smaller subdivisions by means of decimals.

The Second Summary of the Dewey Decimal Classification System is reproduced below.

SECOND SUMMARY OF THE DEWEY DECIMAL CLASSIFICATION SYSTEM[1]
The 100 Divisions

000   Generalities
010   Bibliographies & catalogs
020   Library & information sciences
030   General encyclopedic works
040
050   General serial publications
060   General organizations & museums
070   Journalism, publishing, newspapers
080   General collections
090   Manuscripts & book rarities

100   Philosophy & related disciplines
110   Metaphysics
120   Knowledge, cause, purpose, man
130   Popular & parapsychology, occultism
140   Specific philosophical viewpoints
150   Psychology
160   Logic
170   Ethics (Moral philosophy)
180   Ancient, medieval, Oriental
190   Modern Western philosophy

200   Religion
210   Natural religion
220   Bible
230   Christian doctrinal theology
240   Christian moral & devotional
250   Local church & religious orders
260   Social & ecclesiastical theology
270   History & geography of church
280   Christian denominations & sects
290   Other religions & comparative

300   The social sciences
310   Statistics
320   Political science
330   Economics
340   Law
350   Public administration
360   Social pathology & services

370 Education
380 Commerce
390 Customs & folklore

400 Language
410 Linguistics
420 English & Anglo-Saxon languages
430 Germanic languages   German
440 French, Provençal, Catalan
450 Italian, Romanian, Rhaeto-Romanic
460 Spanish & Portuguese languages
470 Italic languages   Latin
480 Helenic   Classical Greek
490 Other languages

500 Pure sciences
510 Mathematics
520 Astronomy & allied sciences
530 Physics
540 Chemistry & allied sciences
550 Sciences of earth & other worlds
560 Paleontology
570 Life sciences
580 Botanical sciences
590 Zoological sciences

600 Technology (Applied sciences)
610 Medical Sciences
620 Engineering & allied operations
630 Agriculture & related
640 Home economics
650 Managerial services
660 Chemical & related technologies
670 Manufactures
680 Miscellaneous manufactures
690 Buildings

700 The arts
710 Civic & landscape art
720 Architecture
730 Plastic arts   Sculpture
740 Drawing, decorative & minor arts
750 Painting & paintings
760 Graphic arts   Prints
770 Photography & photographs
780 Music
790 Recreational & performing arts

800   Literature (Belles-lettres)
810   American literature in English
820   English & Anglo-Saxon literatures
830   Literatures of Germanic languages
840   French, Provencal, Catalan
850   Italian, Romanian, Rhaeto-Romanic
860   Spanish & Portuguese literatures
870   Italic languages literatures   Latin
880   Hellenic languages literatures
890   Literatures of other languages

900   General geography & history
910   General geography   Travel
920   Biography, genealogy, insignia
930   General history of ancient world
940   General history of Europe
950   General history of Asia
960   General history of Africa
970   General history of North America
980   General history of South America
990   General history of other areas

The Dewey Decimal Classification system begins with 000 (Generalities) and continues through 100 (Philosophy and related disciplines), 300 (Social sciences), 500 (Pure sciences), and 900 (General geography and history). Under 900, 940 is general history of Europe, 970 the general history of North America, and 980 the general history of South America. These numbers can be further subdivided. For example:

973   is for the United States
973.2   Colonial period 1607-1775
973.7   Civil War 1861-1865
973.71   Political and economic history (Civil War period)
973.73   Military operations
973.7349   Battle of Gettysburg
973.9   20th century 1901-
973.92   Later 20th century 1953-

LIBRARY OF CONGRESS CLASSIFICATION SYSTEM

The Library of Congress Classification system was designed by the Library of Congress in the latter part of the 19th century solely for its own use. Because it is so comprehensive, it has been adopted by many other large libraries both in the United States and in other parts of the world. Since one condition of copyright is that the author presents two copies of his work to the Library of Congress, the Library receives copies of every book copyrighted in the United States. In addition, the Library of Congress acquires numerous other publications. Most of these are classified and cataloged by the Library of Congress, and the call numbers are published for the use of anyone wanting to use them. Each book has an individual call number assigned to it, so that there is not as much variation among libraries using this system as with the Dewey Decimal system.

The Library of Congress system, or LC, as it is commonly called, has 21 different classes with numerous subdivisions under each class. Each primary class is designated by a single letter. For example: A is General works; B, Psychology, religion and philosophy; G, Geography, anthropology, and recreation; P, Language and literature; and T, technology. The addition of a second letter indicates a smaller subject under the large subject. For example: AE is for general encyclopedias; BR, Christianity; GC, Oceanography; PE, English language; PR, English literature; and TH, building construction. The K class for law has three letters in some instances. The third letter indicates the state. For example: KFL is Louisiana law; KFT, Texas law; and KFM, Mississippi law. The letter Z is sometimes added to either the one-letter or the two-letter combination to indicate that the book is a bibliography on the subject. Following the first letter or group of letters, each class number has a whole number which indicates a still smaller subdivision. This whole number is often followed by another letter/number combination subdividing the subject even more. For example:

HF	Commerce	HF	Commerce	HF	Commerce
5686	Accounting	5686	Accounting	5686	Accounting
.D7	Drug stores	.P3	Petroleum industry	.S75	Steel industry

Reproduced on the next several pages is a brief outline of the LC system. Although the system is based on the alphabet, not all of the letters have been used in either the main classes or the subclasses. These letters are reserved for new subjects or for the expansion of older subjects. Some libraries with very specialized collections sometimes adapt these unused letters to their own use if the existing class proves inadequate.

LIBRARY OF CONGRESS CLASSIFICATION SYSTEM
CLASSES AND SUBCLASSES[2]

A General Works

AC	Collections. Series. Collected works
AE	Encyclopedias (General)
AG	Dictionaries and other general reference works
AI	Indexes (General)
AM	Museums (General). Collectors and collecting (General)
AN	Newspapers
AP	Periodicals (General)
AS	Academics and learned societies (General)
AY	Yearbooks. Almanacs. Directories
AZ	History of scholarship and learning

[2]U.S. Library of Congress, Subject Cataloging Division, *LC Classification Outline,* 3rd ed. (Washington, D.C.: GPO, 1975).

B Philosophy. Psychology. Religion.

B	Philosophy (General)
BC	Logic
BD	Speculative philosophy
BF	Psychology
BH	Aesthetics
BJ	Ethics
BL	Religions. Mythology. Rationalism
BM	Judaism
BP	Islam. Bahaism. Theosophy, etc.
BQ	Buddhism
BR	Christianity
BS	The Bible and exegesis
BT	Doctrinal theology. Apologetics
BV	Practical theology
BX	Denominations and sects

C Auxiliary Sciences of History

C	Auxiliary sciences of history (General)
CB	History of civilization and culture (General)
CC	Archaeology (General)
CD	Diplomatics. Archives. Seals
CE	Technical chronology. Calendar
CJ	Numismatics
CN	Epigraphy. Inscriptions
CR	Heraldry
CS	Genealogy
CT	Biography

D History: General and Old World

D	History (General)
DA	Great Britain
DB	Austria. Czechoslovakia. Hungary
DC	France
DD	Germany
DE	The Mediterranean region. Greco-Roman world
DF	Greece
DG	Italy
DH-DJ	Netherlands. Belgium. Luxemburg
DK	Russia
DL	Northern Europe. Scandinavia
DP	Spain. Portugal
DQ	Switzerland
DR	Eastern Europe. Balkan Peninsula. Turkey
DS	Asia

DT	Africa
DU	Oceania (South Seas)
DX	Gypsies

E-F History: America

E	America (General)
F	United States local history

G Geography. Anthropology. Recreation

G	Geography (General)
GA	Mathematical geography. Cartography
GB	Physical geography
GC	Oceanography
GF	Human ecology. Anthropogeography
GN	Anthropology
GR	Folklore
GT	Manners and customs (General)
GV	Recreation

H Social Sciences

H	Social sciences (General)
HA	Statistics

Economics

HB	Economic theory
HC	Economic history and conditions. National production
HD	Land. Agriculture. Industry
HE	Transportation and communication
HF	Commerce
HG	Finance
HJ	Public finance

Sociology

HM	Sociology (General and theoretical)
HN	Social history. Social problems. Social reform

Social Groups

HQ	The family. Marriage. Woman
HS	Societies: Secret, benevolent, etc. Clubs
HT	Communities. Classes. Races
HV	Social pathology. Social and public welfare. Criminology
HX	Socialism. Communism. Anarchism

J Political Science

J	Official documents
JA	Collections and general works
JC	Political theory. Theory of state

Constitutional history and administration

JF	General works. Comparative works

Special countries

JK	United States
JL	British America. Latin America
JN	Europe
JQ	Asia. Africa. Australia. Oceania
JS	Local government
JV	Colonies and colonization. Emigration and immigration
JX	International law. International relations

K Law

Law of the United Kingdom and Ireland

KD	Law of England and Wales
KDC	Law of Scotland
KDE	Law of Northern Ireland
KDG	Law of Isle of Man and the Channel Islands
KDK	Law of Ireland (Éire)

Law of the United States

KF	Federal law. Common and collective state law
KFA-KFW	Law of the individual states
KFX	Law of individual cities, A-Z
KFZ	Law of individual territories

L Education

L	Education (General)
LA	History of education
LB	Theory and practice of education
LC	Special aspects of education

Individual institutions: universities, colleges, and schools

LD	United States
LE	America, except United States
LF	Europe
LG	Asia. Africa. Oceania
LH	College and school magazines and papers
LJ	Student fraternities and societies, United States
LT	Textbooks

M Music and Books on Music

M	Music
ML	Literature of music
MT	Music instruction and study

N Fine Arts

N	Visual arts (General)
NA	Architecture
NB	Sculpture
NC	Drawing. Design. Illustration

ND	Painting
NE	Print media
NK	Decorative arts. Applied arts. Decoration and ornament
NX	Arts in general

P Language and Literature

P	Philology and linguistics (General)
PA	Classical languages and literatures
PB	Modern European languages
PC	Romance languages
PD	Germanic languages
PE	English
PF	West Germanic
PG	Slavic. Baltic, Albanian languages and literatures
PH	Finno-Ugrian, Basque languages and literatures
PJ	Oriental languages and literatures
PK	Indo-Iranian
PL	Languages and literatures of Eastern Asia, Africa, Oceania
PM	American Indian languages

Literature

PN	Literary history and collections (General)
PQ	Romance literatures
PR	English literature
PS	American literature
PT	Germanic literatures
PZ	Fiction and juvenile literature

Q Science

Q	Science (General)
QA	Mathematics
QB	Astronomy
QC	Physics
QD	Chemistry
QE	Geology
QH	Natural history (General)
QK	Botany
QL	Zoology
QM	Human anatomy
QP	Physiology
QR	Microbiology

R Medicine

R	Medicine (General)
RA	Public aspects of medicine
RB	Pathology

RC	Internal medicine. Practice of medicine
RD	Surgery
RE	Opthalmology
RF	Otorhinolaryngology
RG	Gynecology and obstetrics
RJ	Pediatrics
RK	Dentistry
RL	Dermatology
RM	Therapeutics. Pharmacology
RS	Pharmacy and materia medica
RT	Nursing
RV	Botanic, Thomsonian, and eclectic medicine
RX	Homeopathy
RZ	Other systems of medicine

S Agriculture

S	Agriculture (General)
SB	Plant culture
SD	Forestry
SF	Animal culture
SH	Aquaculture. Fisheries. Angling
SK	Hunting

T Technology

T	Technology (General)
TA	Engineering (General). Civil engineering (General)
TC	Hydraulic engineering
TD	Environmental technology. Sanitary engineering
TE	Highway engineering. Roads and pavements
TF	Railroad engineering and operation
TG	Bridge engineering
TH	Building construction
TJ	Mechanical engineering and machinery
TK	Electrical engineering. Electronics. Nuclear engineering
TL	Motor vehicles. Aeronautics. Astronautics
TN	Mining engineering. Metallurgy
TP	Chemical technology
TR	Photography
TS	Manufactures
TT	Handicrafts. Arts and crafts
TX	Home economics

U Military Science

U	Military science (General)
UA	Armies: Organization, description, facilities, etc.
UB	Military administration

UC	Maintenance and transportation
UD	Infantry
UE	Cavalry. Armored and mechanized cavalry
UF	Artillery
UG	Military engineering
UH	Other services

V Naval Science

V	Naval science (General)
VA	Navies: Organization, description, facilities, etc.
VB	Naval administration
VC	Naval maintenance
VD	Naval seamen
VE	Marines
VF	Naval ordnance
VG	Minor services of the navies
VK	Navigation. Merchant marine
VM	Naval architecture. Shipbuilding. Marine engineering

Z Bibliography. Library Science

Z	Books in general
4-8	History of books and bookmaking
40-115	Writing
116-549	Book industries and trade
662-1000	Libraries and library science
1001-8999	Bibliography

For most students very little purpose is served by learning all the classes in either the Dewey Decimal or the Library of Congress systems. It is useful, however, for the researcher to learn the class numbers in the Dewey system or the class letters in LC in the particular field in which he is working. This does not eliminate the need to use the card catalog, but it does help in locating books on the shelves.

CALL NUMBERS

The call number assigned to a book indicates its subject matter, author, and location in the library. No two books ever have exactly the same call number. Each call number is distinctive for that book. Multiple copies have a copy number added so that even with several copies there is a slight variation in the call number. For example, if there are three copies of the book with the number $\frac{HD}{6483}$ the first copy usually will not have a copy number. The second and third copies will have c.2 and c.3 added below the number.

In both the Dewey and LC the call number is composed of the *class number* and the *book number*. The class number is the top part of the call number and is derived from the subject matter of the book. Generally, every book on the same subject will have the same class number.

The book number, which is also referred to as the Cutter number, stands for the author of the book and sometimes the title. It is called the Cutter number after Charles A. Cutter who devised a set of tables using the first letter or letters of a name plus a number so that all books with the same class number are together on the shelves, arranged in alphabetical order by the first letter of the author's last name. If the author has written several books on the same subject, then the first letter of the title of the book is added to the Dewey book number. If different editions of a book are issued, the Dewey system usually adds an edition number as part of the book number.

The Library of Congress does not use the Cutter tables, but their book numbers do follow the same basic pattern. The letter stands for the first letter of the author's last name, but the number varies with the book. If an author writes several books on the same subject, instead of adding a letter standing for the title of the book to the book number, the book number is changed. If there are several editions of the same book, the date of the edition is added to the bottom of the call number. For example:

Library of Congress		*Dewey Decimal*
F 369 D24 1971	Davis, Edwin Adams Louisiana; a narrative history. . .1971	976.3 D261La3
F 369 D24 1965	Davis, Edwin Adams Louisiana; a narrative history. . .1965	976.3 D261La2
F 369 D24 1961	Davis, Edwin Adams Louisiana; a narrative history. . .1961	976.3 D261La
F 369 D25 1975	Davis, Edwin Adams Louisiana, the Pelican state. . .1975	976.3 D261L4
F 369 D25 1969	Davis, Edwin Adams Louisiana, the Pelican state. . .c1969	976.3 D261L3

F	Davis, Edwin Adams	976.3
369	Louisiana, the Pelican state. . .c1959	D261L
D25		

F	Davis, Edwin Adams	976.3
369	The story of Louisiana. . .1960	D261s
D26		

When looking for books on the shelves, the same basic techniques are used for both Dewey and LC. In Dewey the number before the decimal point is treated as a whole number. Everything following the decimal point is treated as a decimal. The book number is always a decimal number, even though the decimal does not appear in the number. The following call numbers are arranged in correct order as they would stand on the shelves:

338	338	338.908	338.91	338.917	338.917	338.94
A221i	A36	F911r	B185e	R896y	R9	R31c

In locating a call number in LC, it is necessary to start with the letter or letter combination and then proceed to the numbers. As with Dewey, the first set of numbers is treated as a whole number. The whole number will be followed either with a decimal point or another letter/number combination. These remaining numbers are all treated as decimals. For example, the following call numbers are arranged in correct order as they would stand on the shelves:

PN	PN	PN	PN	PN
6	56	56	56.3	Z
S55	.H63T5	.H63T5	N4J6	6940
		1967	1971	P69

Many libraries have books housed in areas other than the regular stacks, and these areas are usually indicated by a symbol over the call number. For example, books on the reference shelves often will have the symbols R, Ref, or X. It is necessary to check the library handbook or a chart of symbols to determine their meaning and location.

5
CARD CATALOG

The card catalog is the index to all of the cataloged and classified materials in the library. This includes the books, reference books, some pamphlets, and often the periodicals. However, some libraries prefer to list their periodicals in a separate file. If they are included in the card catalog, the "holdings" usually are not listed. For example, the card catalog normally will not indicate whether or not the library owns the December 1977 issue of the *National Geographic* magazine. It tells, however, that the library does subscribe to the magazine and when the magazine began publication, and it gives its call number or location. To determine the holdings it is necessary to check the record of periodicals received by the library.

Many libraries have dictionary-type catalogs consisting of multiple drawers containing 3 × 5 cards arranged alphabetically by author, title, subject, and added entries. Added entries consist of cards for such things as editors, compilers, translators, illustrators, arrangers of music, and series. Some dictionary-type catalogs are divided into sections and are referred to as *divided* catalogs. Some divided catalogs consist of 3 sections: author, title, and subject. Others consist of 2 sections: author and title/subject. Whatever the arrangement, the cards are filed alphabetically within each section.

Early libraries often used *book catalogs* which listed the library's holdings in book form. It was difficult to keep these catalogs up-to-date, and it was necessary to issue frequent supplements. Because of the ease with which computer-generated materials can be reproduced, some libraries are going back to the book catalog. Usually these are relatively small libraries such as a company library, one affiliated with a research organization, or a library having several branches. With a book catalog it is rather easy to maintain several catalogs at the same time in different locations. The "up-dates" are kept in a separate volume until complete revisions are made. The library patron must consult several different volumes to be sure that he is getting all the references.

In some libraries the card catalog is being abandoned completely, and computer terminals are being installed to take its place. However, these are expensive to install and maintain and are often difficult for the library patron to use. There is the added problem of providing enough terminals so that patrons will have ready access to them. Computer terminals provide for rapid information retrieval and are especially good for the serious scholar who wants everything the library has on a particular subject. Some libraries belong to information retrieval networks that allow the library patron to see what other libraries have in his field of study. Access to the network usually is not provided as a free service, and charges are made for each inquiry.

CARDS IN THE CARD CATALOG

Practically every book, with the exception of fiction, has at least three cards in the catalog. These are: the author, or main entry card; the title card; and one or more subject cards. Many books also have several added entry cards, such as: joint author, editor, compiler, arranger (music), translator (important in languages, literature, and the sciences), illustrator, or series. The author card is often referred to as the "main entry." Before printed cards were in wide usage, catalog cards were either handwritten or typed, a time-consuming and, therefore, expensive process. To reduce this expense, the author card was the only card to have the complete bibliographical information; the other cards were abbreviated. For this reason, to get all the needed bibliographical information it was necessary to go back to the author card. Thus, the author card was referred to as the "main entry." With printed cards, except for the top line, all the cards are identical. The author card is still referred to as the "main entry" although its original meaning is no longer valid.

Learning to interpret the material on the catalog card is one of the most important and useful skills that the library user can acquire. The card catalog provides the location of materials for research papers and all the needed bibliographical information such as the full name of the author, complete title of the book, edition, and imprint. Of course, this information is usually available from the book itself, but it is more efficient to get it from the catalog card. The catalog card also suggests other related subject headings under which additional material can be found.

On the following pages are some of the more common kinds of cards found in the card catalog.

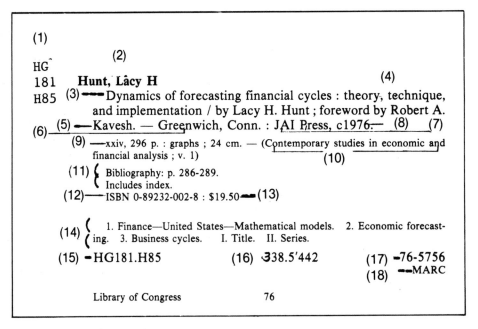

Figure 5-1. Author card.

(1)   Call number for the book. It is always found in the upper left corner of the card. This book is classified in the Library of Congress Classification system.

(2)   Author of the book. On some cards dates after the author's name indicate the year of birth and sometimes death date. On newer cards this is often omitted because of the high cost of determining this information.

(3)   Short-title of the book.

(4)   Sub-title or explanatory title. This is combined with the short-title to form the complete title. The complete title is necessary for bibliographical purposes.

(5)   Sometimes the foreword or introduction is written by the author. In this instance it was written by someone else.

(6)   Place of publication. Occasionally more than one place is indicated.

(7)   Publisher of the book. If more than one publisher is given, it usually indicates that the book is a reprint or a foreign publication that has been published also in this country.

(8)   Copyright date. The publication date is often given instead of the copyright date. It is written without the small "c" in front of the date. Sometimes both dates are given. For example: c1976, 1977.

(9)   Physical description. This includes the number of preliminary pages, number of pages of text, kinds of illustrations if any, and the height of the book. This book has 24 preliminary pages numbered in small Roman numerals, 296 pages of text numbered in Arabic numerals, and an unspecified number of graphs. It is 24 centimeters tall.

(10)   Series note or series notation. This book is volume 1 of the *Contemporary Studies in Economic and Financial Analysis* series.

(11)   This area is reserved for any special notes that the cataloger wants to bring to the attention of the reader. This book has a bibliography and an index.

(12)   International Standard Book Number

(13)   Price of the book. The price is not always given, and sometimes it follows the physical description.

(14)   Tracings. The *tracings* are a record kept by the library of the kinds and number of cards in the card catalog for that particular book. Items indicated by the Arabic numerals are the subject headings and tell the reader the subject matter covered as well as the specific subject headings to use to find other books on the same subject. The Roman numerals indicate added entry cards such as joint authors, title, illustrators, editors, and sometimes series.

(15)   Library of Congress call number.

(16)   Dewey Decimal class number. Since the book number sometimes varies from library to library, only the class number is given. Each library assigns its own book number.

(17)   Order number used by libraries to order cards for this book from the Library of Congress.

(18)   Indicates that this is a Machine Readable Card.

```
HG          Dynamics of forecasting financial cycles
181         Hunt, Lacy H
H85             Dynamics of forecasting financial cycles : theory, technique,
            and implementation / by Lacy H. Hunt ; foreword by Robert A.
            Kavesh. — Greenwich, Conn. : JAI Press, c1976.

                xxiv, 296 p. : graphs ; 24 cm. — (Contemporary studies in economic and
            financial analysis ; v. 1)

                Bibliography: p. 286-289.
                Includes index.
                ISBN 0-89232-002-8 : $19.50


                1. Finance—United States—Mathematical models.    2. Economic forecast-
            ing.   3. Business cycles.    I. Title.   II. Series.

            HG181.H85                    338.5'442                    76-5756
                                                                      MARC


            Library of Congress              76
```

Figure 5-2. Title card.

The title card is exactly the same as the author card except that the title is typed on the top of the card above the author's name. The title of the book is repeated under the author's name.

```
HG          FINANCE--UNITED STATES--MATHEMATICAL MODELS
181         Hunt, Lacy H
H85             Dynamics of forecasting financial cycles : theory, technique,
            and implementation / by Lacy H. Hunt ; foreword by Robert A.
            Kavesh. — Greenwich, Conn. : JAI Press, c1976.

                xxiv, 296 p. : graphs ; 24 cm. — (Contemporary studies in economic and
            financial analysis ; v. 1)

                Bibliography: p. 286-289.
                Includes index.
                ISBN 0-89232-002-8 : $19.50


                1. Finance—United States—Mathematical models.    2. Economic forecast-
            ing.   3. Business cycles.    I. Title.   II. Series.

            HG181.H85                    338.5'442                    76-5756
                                                                      MARC


            Library of Congress              76
```

Figure 5-3. Subject card.

Subject cards have the subject typed above the author's name in either black capitals or red type. This varies from library to library, and some card catalogs will have both. The newer method is the black capitals. This book has three subject cards in the catalog.

PN 4177 R44

The **Reference** shelf. v. 1–
New York, H. W. Wilson Co. [1922–

v. illus. 19–21 cm.

Some numbers in rev. editions.

1. Debates and debating—Collections.

*808.53   58–13997 ‡

Library of Congress   [5]

Figure 5-4. Cover card for a series.

PN 4177 R44

The Reference shelf.   (Card 78

Contents cont'd:

v.49,no.1Canada in transition. 1977.
v.49,no.2The death penalty. 1977.
v.49,no.3The struggle against terrorism. 1977.
v.49,no.4See v. 11, no. 10.
v.49,no.5Women and men. 1977.
v.49,no.6Religions in America. 1977.

v.50,no.1Medical care in the United States. 1978.

Figure 5-5. Contents card for a series.

PN
4177   **Canada in transition** / edited by Grant S. McClellan. — New York
R44   : H. W. Wilson, 1977.
v. 49   224 p. : map ; 19 cm. — (The Reference shelf ; v. 49, no. 1)
no. 1   Bibliography: p. 216-224.
        SUMMARY: A series of articles dealing with the changing economic, poli-
    tical, and social aspects of present-day Canada and the influence of an emerging
    spirit of nationalism.
        ISBN 0-8242-0603-7

                                                                (Continued on next card)
                                                                    77-951
                                                                    MARC
                            77   AC

Figure 5-6a. Card for individual title in a series.

PN
4177   **Canada in transition ... 1977.   (Card 2)**
R44
v. 49
no. 1   1. Canada—Politics and government—1945-   —Addresses, essays, lec-
    tures. 2. Canada—Economic conditions—1945-   —Addresses, essays,
    lectures. 3. Canada—Foreign relations—1945-   —Addresses, essays,
    lectures. 4. Québec (Province)—History—Autonomy and independence
    movements—Addresses, essays. lectures. I. McClellan,
    Grant S. II. Series.

        F1034.2.C29   320.9'71'064   77-951
                                                        MARC

        Library of Congress   77   AC

Figure 5-6b. Continuation of individual title in a series.

    Many books are part of a series and may be located in the card catalog under the name of
the series, subject of the series, or the author, title, and subject of each book in the series.

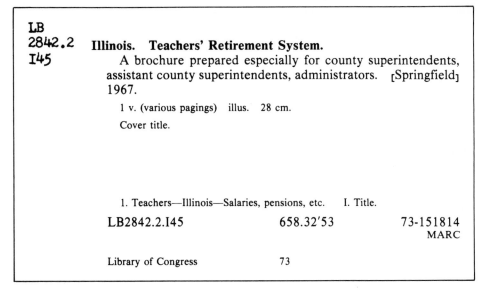

```
LB
2842.2    Illinois.  Teachers' Retirement System.
I45              A brochure prepared especially for county superintendents,
           assistant county superintendents, administrators.  [Springfield]
           1967.
                1 v. (various pagings)   illus.   28 cm.
                Cover title.




                1. Teachers—Illinois—Salaries, pensions, etc.   I. Title.
           LB2842.2.I45                 658.32'53              73-151814
                                                                    MARC

                Library of Congress              73
```

Figure 5-7. Corporate entry.

The corporate entry or corporate author refers to an organization such as a governmental agency, an association, or a company that issues a publication in its name rather than in the name of the person or persons who did the actual writing. The author or perhaps several joint authors have done the writing as part of their assigned duties, but the book is the responsibility of the issuing agency. Often with publications from the United States government, both the corporate author and the personal author are given.

On this card the publisher is not indicated. The Illinois Teachers' Retirement System is the publisher as well as the corporate author, and this information is not repeated.

```
V Med
SF
745      The Merck veterinary manual; a handbook of diagnosis and
M4           therapy for the veterinarian.  O. H. Siegmund, editor.  4th
1973         ed.  Rahway, N. J., Merck, 1973.
                xii, 1618 p.   18 cm.
                Pages [1601]-1618 blank for "Notes."



                1. Veterinary medicine—Handbooks, manuals, etc.   I. Siegmund,
           O. H., ed.   II. Merck and Company, Inc.
           SF745.M4   1973              636.089'6              73-174840
           ISBN 0-911910-51-4                                      MARC
```

Figure 5-8. Title entry as main entry.

With reference books that are well-known by title and which are reissued at frequent intervals, the main entry is often the title entry. Many times the editors differ from edition to edition. It is easier to find all the editions of the work together in the card catalog under title rather than under several different editors.

Figure 5-9 is an example of a book in which each chapter has been written by a different person. The chapters were compiled and edited by someone else. Because the editor bears the responsibility for the work, it is entered under his name.

Two different imprints are indicated on this card: Chicago, A.W. Shaw, 1927 and New York, J.S. Ozer, 1971. This means that the book was reprinted forty-four years after the first printing but was not changed in content. The second imprint is placed in brackets [ ] because it does not appear on the title page of the book, but has been supplied by the cataloger either from some other section of the book such as the verso of the title page or from an outside bibliographic source such as *Cumulative Book Index*.

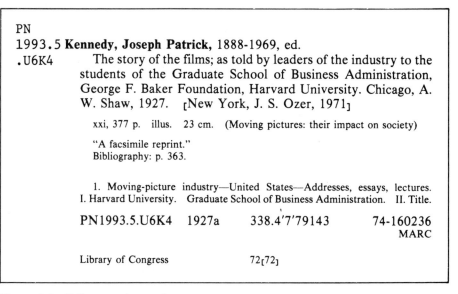

Figure 5-9. Editor used as author.

Periodicals are listed in the card catalog by title, subject, and sometimes by the first editor. Periodical cards differ from other cards in the catalog in that they give the title of the magazine, volume 1-, and the date of volume 1 on the author line. In the example shown in figure 5-10, the date of the first issue of volume 1 is May 1885. The dash after both the volume number and the date indicates that the periodical is still being published. If it ceases publication, the number of the last volume and the date would be added to the card.

There is one subject heading given for this periodical. If the reader is interested in finding other periodicals on the subject of "home economics," he should look in the card catalog under the subject heading—HOME ECONOMICS-PERIODICALS. He will find a card for *Good Housekeeping* and all the other periodicals that the library has on this subject.

```
TX        Good housekeeping ...   v. 1–
 1          May 1885–
G7         Holyoke, Mass., and New York city, C. W. Bryan & co.;
           ₍etc., etc.₎ 1885–19

                 v.  illus. (part col.) plates, ports.   25 cm. (v. 1–11: 30½ cm.)

           Biweekly, 1885–90; monthly, 1891–
           From Oct. 1909 to Apr. 1916 title reads: Good housekeeping maga-
           zine.
           Published in Holyoke, Mass., and New York, 1885–86; Springfield,
           Mass., 1886–1910; New York, 1911–

           1. Domestic economy—Period.

           TX1.G7                                          8—37003

           Library of Congress              ₍62r26w½₎
```

Figure 5-10. Card for periodical.

Many periodical publishers have branched out into the book publishing business, and the name of the periodical is used as a corporate author. This causes much confusion for card catalog users. This confusion can be eliminated if the reader remembers that the card for the periodical is similar to the card pictured in Figure 5-10. It has the title of the periodical, volume 1-, and the date of volume 1 on the author line. Occasionally the holdings are given on a second and perhaps a third card. On the other hand, the card for the book has the name of the periodical as a corporate author on the author line and the title of the book on the title line. Both kinds of cards have imprint, physical description, and tracings.

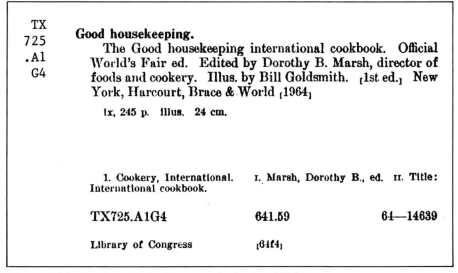

```
TX        Good housekeeping.
725         The Good housekeeping international cookbook.  Official
.A1        World's Fair ed.  Edited by Dorothy B. Marsh, director of
G4         foods and cookery.  Illus. by Bill Goldsmith.  ₍1st ed.₎  New
           York, Harcourt, Brace & World ₍1964₎

           ix, 245 p.  illus.  24 cm.

           1. Cookery, International.   ɪ. Marsh, Dorothy B., ed.   ɪɪ. Title:
           International cookbook.

           TX725.A1G4             641.59             64—14639

           Library of Congress           ₍64f4₎
```

Figure 5-11. Book published by a periodical publisher.

```
Film       Washington post.  Dec.6, 1877-
30         Washington, D.C.

           Microfilm.  Positive.
           Collation of the original:   v. illus.,
      ports.    daily.
           Many slight variations in title.


      1.  Newspapers - Washington, D.C.
```

Figure 5-12. Newspaper card.

Because newspapers are very bulky to store, constitute a fire hazard, and are printed on rather poor quality paper that deteriorates quite rapidly, many libraries have them put on microfilm or buy microfilm copies of the paper. Microfilming eliminates the disadvantages and gives the library a permanent copy of the paper. The only date on the card (Figure 5-12) is the beginning date of the newspaper, Dec. 6, 1877-. This implies that the library has microfilm copies of the *Washington Post* dating back to 1877. Incomplete holdings usually are noted on the card. Some libraries give the complete holdings, but in most libraries it is necessary to consult the newspaper acquisition list for such information. To locate an issue of this newspaper, it is necessary to know the film number and the date of the issue desired. Usually the film number is the same for all issues of the title.

Non-published Materials

Many libraries have a vast amount of material in nonbook form such as films, microforms, records, reel-to-reel tapes, cassettes, and scores. Sometimes the cards for these materials are kept in a separate file, but many times they are inter-filed in the card catalog along with all other materials. Since these generally are kept in a separate collection, they usually have a location symbol such as "Film," "LP," "Recording," or "Tape" plus a sequence number instead of a classification number as a means of locating them. The number given with the location symbol is often an accession number. This means that as the materials are received by the library, they are assigned a number indicating their order of receipt. Sometimes a classification number and a location symbol are assigned to non-book materials.

When writing research papers, it is often useful to listen to a recording of a play, an excerpt from a novel, or a poem being read by a famous performer such as Sir Laurence Olivier. Recordings of great events in history such as the landing on the moon, speeches given by outstanding historical figures such as Sir Winston Churchill, songs of birds recorded in certain areas, or sounds of marine animals recorded in their native environment are available in college and university libraries and add much interest to research papers.

The recording noted in Figure 5-13 would be useful to the student studying the portrayal of Jesus Christ in fiction. Perhaps the student would be interested in the performer, Elise Bell, or the works of Elizabeth G. Spears, author of the original book.

```
LP        Bell, Elise.
5746          The bronze bow.  [Phonodisc]  Based on the book by
          Elizabeth George Speare.  Newbery Award Records NAR
          3029.  [1972]

              2 s.  12 in.  33⅓ rpm.

              "A recorded dramatization of the Newbery medal award book."
              Duration : 42 min., 53 sec.
              Notes by R. Van Gelder on slipcase.


                 [1. Jesus Christ—Fiction.   2. Palestine—Fiction]      I. Speare,
              Elizabeth George.  The bronze bow.  II. Title.

              [PZ7]                                              73–760797

              Library of Congress            73 [2]                      MN
```

Figure 5-13. Card for a recording.

Musical scores frequently are cataloged and the cards filed in the card catalog with books and other materials. The main entry in Figure 5-14 is the composer, but it is also possible to locate the score by subject and title. In some libraries the scores are shelved together in the stacks by call number, while in other libraries they are housed in separate collections. If they are housed in a separate collection, they usually have a location symbol plus the call number or perhaps just the location symbol.

```
M         Kelly, Bryan.
1247
K24           March—Washington D. C.  London, Novello [1971]
                 score (26 p.) and      parts.  28 cm.  (Novello brass band series)
                 Duration : 4 min., 30 sec.




                 1. Marches (Band)—Scores and parts.   I. Title.   II. Title:
              Washington D. C.

              M1247.K                                          79–295315

              Library of Congress         71 [2]                       M
```

Figure 5-14. Catalog card for a score.

A thesis is a long treatise or scholarly research paper written in partial fulfillment for the master's degree. The dissertation is similar but represents original work which is written in partial fulfillment of the requirements for the doctoral degree. Theses and dissertations are usually unpublished and, therefore, do not have an imprint except for the date. The one in Figure 5-15 is available in its original form shelved by the call number and is also on microfilm.

```
378.76    Lee, Anthony, 1951-
L930          Analysis of a chilling system used
1936      for extrusion coating of paper / by
          Anthony Lee. [Baton Rouge : s.n.] ,
Also on   1976.
Film          x, 50 leaves : ill. ; 29 cm.
              Thesis (M.S. in M.E.)--Louisiana
          State University, Baton Rouge, La.
              Vita.
              Bibliography:  leaves 41-42.
              Abstract.
              1.  Paper coatings. I. Title
```

Figure 5-15. Thesis on microfilm.

Cross Reference or Directional Cards

The cards that have been discussed so far in this chapter describe books, periodicals, newspapers, and non-book materials and tell how they can be located. Cross reference cards direct the card catalog user to the proper terminology or to additional sources of information. There are two kinds of cross reference cards—*see* and *see also*. The *see* reference directs the card catalog user from a subject heading or term that is not used to the synonymous term that is used. The *see also* reference card lists related subject headings under which more information can be found.

The *subject cross* reference in Figure 5-16 indicates that JET FUEL is not used as a subject heading and that JET PLANES—FUEL is used instead. The cross reference card is filed in the card catalog in the correct place alphabetically by the first line on the card.

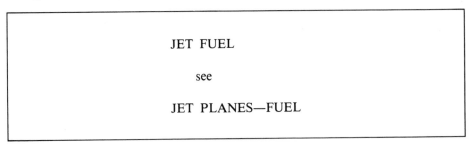

JET FUEL

see

JET PLANES—FUEL

Figure 5-16. Subject cross reference.

A *name cross* reference is used to direct the card catalog user from the pen name or pseudonym of the author to the author's real name. Some card catalogs have such works entered under both names making the name cross reference card unnecessary.

```
Henry, O., pseud.

           see

Porter, William Sydney, 1862-1910
```

Figure 5-17. Name cross reference.

The *see also* card indicates subject headings under which additional information can be found. These are filed after the last card with the same subject heading. For example, there might be fifteen cards in the card catalog with the simple subject heading, KINDERGARTEN. The sixteenth card would be the one noted below. The seventeenth card might be KINDER-GARTEN—AIMS AND OBJECTIVES.

```
KINDERGARTEN

see also Child study; Montessori method of education; nursery schools
```

Figure 5-18. *See also* reference.

ARRANGEMENT OF THE CARD CATALOG

Two methods of filing are commonly used in indexes and card catalogs. They are *letter by letter* and *word by word*. Dictionaries use letter by letter filing as do some indexes and encyclopedias. Cards in the card catalog are filed word by word. The student should be aware of differences in the two methods so that he will not miss entries in reference sources. The word by word method treats each word in a name, title, or subject heading as a separate unit while the letter by letter method treats all the words in a name, title, or subject heading as if they were one unit. In other words, in the letter by letter method all the words are run together as if they were one word. For example:

Word by Word	Letter by Letter
San Antonio	San Antonio
San Diego	Sanctuary
San Pedro	Sandalwood
Sanctuary	Sand blasting
Sand blasting	Sand, George
Sand, George	San Diego
Sandalwood	San Pedro

The dictionary-type card catalog has the cards arranged in alphabetical order, so it is necessary to find the section of the catalog that contains the correct part of the alphabet. Each drawer has a label indicating the parts of the alphabet included in that drawer. Quite often the drawers are numbered so that they can be returned to their cases in proper order. Within each drawer there are guide cards which indicate the contents of various sections of that drawer. If there is not a guide card with the subject printed across the top, it does not mean that the library does not have books on that topic. Guide cards are used to indicate only some of the subjects found in the drawer.

Filing Rules

1. All filing is done by the first line on the catalog card.
2. An author's name or a personal name used as a subject is inverted. Example: *Lindbergh, Anne Morrow* not *Anne Morrow Lindbergh.*
3. Several books by the same author are filed first under the author's name and then alphabetically by title. Example:
   Colby, Carroll Burleigh. *FBI . . .*
   Colby, Carroll Burleigh. *Sailing Ships . . .*
   Colby, Carroll Burleigh. *Wild Bird World.*
4. Several authors with the same last name are filed first by last name and then alphabetically by the first and middle name. If the entire name is the same, then the names are listed chronologically by year of birth. Royalty is listed chronologically by number. Example:
   Gillespie, George, 1613-1648.
   Gillespie, George, 1683-1760.
   Gillespie, George Benjamin, 1863-
   Henry II, King of England, 1133-1189.
   Henry III, King of England, 1207-1272.
   Henry IV, King of England, 1367-1413.
5. Compound personal names are filed as though they were one word. Example: Armstrong, Martin D. is filed before Armstrong-Jones, Anthony.
6. Compound names are arranged as separate words whether or not they are separated by a hyphen. This includes names beginning with New, Old, West, South, Saint, San, etc. Example: New Zealand is filed before Newcastle.

7. Titles are filed under the first word of the title unless the title begins with *a, an,* or *the.* With foreign book titles, the foreign equivalents of the English articles are ignored and are filed by the next word. Example: *The Great Gatsby* is filed under *Great,* and *Les Miserables* is filed under *Miserables.* If the title of a book is not distinctive such as *Collected works of . . .* or *Outline of . . .,* there is no title card. When the title is the same as a standardized subject heading, the subject card substitutes for the title card. This is particularly true with biographies.

8. Compound words are arranged as one word. Example: *Silversmith* is filed after *Silver question.*

9. Dates are filed as they are commonly spoken. Example: *1848: The Fall of Metternich* is filed under eighteen forty-eight. . . .

10. Numbers are filed as if they are spelled out except where numerical or chronological order is necessary. Example: *1001 Questions Answered about the Mineral Kingdom* would be filed as one thousand one questions . . ., but the subject heading *Italian literature—14th century* would be filed after *Italian literature—13th century* and before *Italian literature— 15th century.*

11. Abbreviations are filed as if spelled out in full. Example: Dr. Schweitzer as *Doctor* Schweitzer, St. Louis as *Saint* Louis, and N.Y. as *New York.*

12. Initials and acronyms are arranged at the beginning of the appropriate letter and before any words beginning with that letter. Example: COBOL (computer program language) would be filed where the letter "C" begins in the drawer and before Cable, A.J.

13. Names beginning with M', Mc, and Mac are all filed as if spelled "Mac." Example: McCulloch, Machine, M'Nulty, and MacPherson are arranged in correct order.

14. Modified letters such as the umlaut ä, ö, ü are arranged as if written ae, oe, and ue. Example: Müller, Erich Herman is filed before Muller, C.F.J.

15. Hyphenated words are arranged as separate words. Example: part-time is filed before participant.

16. All punctuation marks are disregarded. Example: O'Neal, Hank; Oneal, James; O'Neal, Leland.

Since card catalogs vary somewhat from library to library, the card catalog user should study the library handbook in that particular library to see what its filing practices are. Also since some dates, names, and initials are sometimes filed rather peculiarly, it is a good idea to look elsewhere in the catalog than in the place one would logically expect to find them. For example: UNESCO is filed as a word rather than as an acronym. Sometimes it is very difficult to tell from context how things should be filed. If the student remembers the different possibilities, his search will be more successful.

Subject Headings

Many users of the card catalog are not familiar with authors or titles of books and, therefore, must look for material by subject. Looking for information by subject can be confusing because the card catalog user may not be familiar with the terminology. Organizations such as the American Library Association, H.W. Wilson Co., and the Library of Congress have published lists of standardized subject headings which are used extensively in card catalogs and indexes. Libraries and publishers of indexes and other reference materials use these standardized subject headings to promote uniformity among reference sources. Many times individual libraries and individual publishers add other subject headings to fit their particular needs, but the basic format remains the same.

The primary rule in looking for subject headings is to proceed from the specific to the general. The card catalog user should think of the topic as precisely as possible and try to determine the subject heading that would be the most appropriate. For example, to locate material on educating the blind, the student finds that the subject heading *Education* is too broad. Instead, he should look under the more precise subject heading *Blind—Education*. Skill in selecting the proper subject heading requires much practice and some imagination.

If the library user is unable to find material in the card catalog on a topic, perhaps he is using the wrong subject headings. To check the accuracy of a subject heading and to get suggestions, he should consult the *Library of Congress Subject Headings* (8th ed., 1975) for additional references. This is a two-volume work published by the Library of Congress and commonly referred to as the "LC List of Subject Headings." It lists subject headings used by the Library of Congress in their catalogs, as well as *see* references for terms not used, and *see also* references for related topics. Many libraries follow the practices used by the Library of Congress but add their own subject headings to fulfill special local needs.

There are three kinds of subject headings: *simple, inverted,* and *divided.* The *simple* subject heading is one word or a phrase; for example, *Photography* or *Photography in oceanography.* The simple subject heading is used for books of a general nature or for subjects too specialized to be sub-divided.

The *inverted* subject heading is a simple phrase subject heading which has been reversed for purposes of alphabetizing. It is desirable to have all aspects of a topic together in one area of the catalog. To accomplish this the key word or the noun is listed first followed by the adjective; for example, *Photography, Commercial* or *Photography, Trick.* Thus, "commercial photography" and "trick photography" are filed with other books on photography.

The *divided* subject heading is used to indicate more precisely the content and sometimes the form of a book than is possible with either the simple or inverted subject headings; for example, *Photography—United States—History—Bibliography* or *Photography—Dictionaries.* The first example indicates that the book is a bibliography, or a list of sources, on the history of photography in the United States. "United States" is a *geographical* subdivision and indicates that the book is limited to this country. "History" is a *special subject* or *topical* subdivision and indicates that the book is not on new developments in photography but reviews past developments. "Bibliography" is an example of a *form* subdivision. A *form* subdivision indicates the type or format of the book. If the student is interested in finding a book which discusses the history of photography in the United States, he would not select a bibliography. He would select, instead, a book having either "handbook," "encyclopedia," or no form subdivision. *Photography-Dictionaries* is a divided subject heading but has fewer sub-divisions. If definitions of terms used in photography are needed, this would be a good choice.

Certain subdivisions are common to all countries, for example:

United States—Antiquities
United States—Economic conditions
United States—Foreign relations
United States—History
United States—Politics and government
United States—Social conditions
United States—Social life and customs

Literature, language, poetry, and drama are entered under the name of the language, for example:

American drama
American literature—Revolutionary period, 1775-1783
American literature—1783-1850
American literature—19th century
American literature—20th century
American poetry

The material under American literature is arranged chronologically. The alphabetical arrangement is ignored when dates follow the subject heading.

Some subject headings are entered under the subject rather than the place of origin. For example, art, architecture, and music are entered in the card catalog as inverted subject headings.

Art, American
Architecture, American
Music, American

Because of the complexities of forms used in subject headings, the library user should check all possible forms of a subject as well as the *Library of Congress Subject Headings* before deciding that the library has nothing on his subject.

THINGS THAT ARE NOT FOUND IN THE CARD CATALOG

To use the card catalog efficiently, the library user must know what he cannot expect to find there, as well as what he can. It is also important for him to know the tools that will enable him to find materials not listed in the card catalog.

Most card catalogs do not have analytic cards for anthologies. Anthologies are collections of literary works such as a group of plays, poems, speeches, short stories, or essays published in a single work. If these collections are analyzed, a set of cards is put in the card catalog indicating the anthology in which the play, poem, short story, speech, or essay is found. Because this is so expensive, most anthologies are not analyzed in the card catalog. The contents of anthologies are listed in indexes to literature in collections, such as: *Play Index, Granger's Index to Poetry, Speech Index, Short Story Index,* and *Essay and General Literature Index.*

Individual articles from periodicals and newspapers are not listed in the card catalog. These are listed in indexes such as *Readers' Guide to Periodical Literature, Humanities Index, Psychological Abstracts,* or *The New York Times Index.*

Libraries which serve as depository libraries for United States government publications usually do not list the contents of the collection in the card catalog. To locate these materials it is necessary to consult such publications as the *Monthly Catalog of U.S. Government Publications, Index to U.S. Government Periodicals,* or the *Congressional Information Service, CIS Annual.*

Supplements to the card catalog will be discussed in more detail in subsequent chapters.

6

REFERENCE BOOKS

The Reference Collection is a vital part of any library. Reference materials usually are located in a special room or area of the library and do not circulate so that they are available when needed. Reference sources generally are those designed to answer a question or give a particular fact and as a rule are not read throughout. There are two categories of reference books: (1) *general* reference books, which include many subjects such as the *Encyclopedia Americana,* and (2) *subject* reference books, which cover one subject such as *Encyclopedia of World Art* or *McGraw-Hill Encyclopedia of Science and Technology.* Reference books also differ in their purpose. Some reference books contain information. Examples of these are dictionaries, encyclopedias, biographical dictionaries, handbooks, gazetteers, and atlases. Other reference sources indicate where the information can be found. Examples of these are indexes, concordances, and bibliographies.

Much valuable time can be saved in the use of reference books if certain characteristics of reference materials are noted.

Date and Scope

One of the first things to consider in examining reference materials is the date and the scope. The copyright date on the back or verso of the title page indicates how recent the information is. Much time can be spent uselessly by looking in an out-of-date book for recent information. The preface will indicate the author's purpose in writing the book and give the scope or range of material covered.

Arrangement

Reference books usually are arranged alphabetically. If the arrangement is not alphabetical, there is an index to lead the reader to the materials included in the book. Many alphabetically arranged books also have indexes. Information is given under large subjects with small subjects listed under the major heading. Some reference sources are chronologically arranged. This is particularly true of histories.

Authority

Many reference books contain articles written by authorities. Each author signs the article either with his complete name or initials. The identification of the initials can be found in a particular place in the book or in one volume of a multivolume set. A signed article is usually an indication of reliable information.

Bibliographies and Cross References

Some reference sources include a bibliography at the end of the article which leads the reader to other materials. Cross references direct the user to a synonymous subject (*see*) or to additional information (*see also*). Another type of cross reference, q.v. (*which see*), is used in some reference sources.

Locating a Reference Book

To find a reference book on a particular subject when the title is not known, the library user should look in the card catalog for the subject with a subdivision such as "encyclopedia," "yearbook," "handbook," or other form subdivisions. One might also search the reference shelves by the call number of the subject for other books. Guides to reference books such as the following also might be consulted.

GUIDES TO REFERENCE BOOKS

Sheehy, Eugene P. Guide to Reference Books. 9th ed. Chicago: American Library Association, 1976.

> A revised and updated version of the 8th edition of Constance M. Winchell's Guide to Reference Books, 1967. The book includes English language and foreign reference materials with all entries annotated. Entries are under major headings: "General Reference Works," "The Humanities," "Social Sciences," "History and Area Studies," "Pure and Applied Sciences." Each group is subdivided by specific type of work, by subject, and/or by country.

Walford, Albert J., ed. Guide to Reference Material. 2d. ed. 3 vols. London: Library Association, 1966-1970.

> Emphasis on British publications. Also provides reference sources international in scope.

DICTIONARIES

A *dictionary,* in its original meaning, is a book that contains the words of a language with their definitions. There are other kinds of dictionaries such as dictionaries of slang, politics, history, art, music, science, biography, and many others. If one is researching an unfamiliar subject, a dictionary devoted to that subject will provide pertinent information.

A dictionary gives information about words—spelling, pronunciation, meaning, derivation, usage, synonyms, and antonyms. An *unabridged* dictionary includes all words in the language with all their definitions including scientific terms. An *abridged* dictionary is a shortened version of an unabridged dictionary. Two widely used unabridged American dictionaries are *Webster's New International Dictionary* and *Funk & Wagnalls New Standard Dictionary. Webster's New Collegiate Dictionary* is an example of an abridged dictionary.

In a dictionary one can find whether a word is no longer in use or has specialized uses. Other features of a dictionary are short biographical facts for well-known people, identification of fictional characters, and geographical locations such as countries, states, and cities. A guide to pronunciation and a list of abbreviations appear in the front of the dictionary. In some dictionaries an *addenda* indicates new words added since the last printing.

General Dictionaries

Unabridged

Webster's Third New International Dictionary of the English Language. Springfield, Mass.: Merriam, 1976.

> This edition includes some 450,000 entries. In the regular alphabet are many new words. The new edition is particularly strong in modern scientific and technical words.

Funk & Wagnalls New Standard Dictionary. New York: Funk & Wagnalls, 1964.

> Features current meanings, spellings, and pronunciations. English words are in one alphabet with a special section for foreign words and phrases.

The Random House Dictionary of the English Language. New York: Random House, 1973.

> An up-to-date and manageable unabridged dictionary. Special features include: four bilingual lists; a color atlas section; lists of countries of the world, states of the United States, and continents; a list of American and foreign colleges and univerisities; and a chronology of important dates in world history.

Abridged

The Random House College Dictionary. New York: Random House, 1975.
Webster's New Collegiate Dictionary. Springfield, Mass.: Merriam, 1977.
Webster's New World Dictionary of the American Language. College ed. Cleveland: Collins-World, 1976.

Historical Dictionaries

Oxford English Dictionary. 12 vols. and supplement. Oxford: Clarendon Press, 1933.

> A scholarly dictionary, giving the history of English words from the twelfth century to the present day. Quotations show how words were used at different periods. The OED, as the dictionary is usually called, is a reissue of Murray's New English Dictionary on Historical Principles.

————. A Supplement to the Oxford English Dictionary. Ed. R.W. Burchfield. 1 vol. (to be completed in 3 vols.) Oxford: Clarendon Press, 1972.

> Contents: vol. 1, A-G.

Craigie, Sir William A., and James R. Hulbert. A Dictionary of American English on Historical Principles. 4 vols. Chicago: University of Chicago Press, 1936-1944.

> Gives the history of English words used in the United States from Colonial times to the end of the 19th century. Also includes words and phrases of purely American origin. Many quotations are given to illustrate word usage.

Foreign Language Dictionaries

Harrap's New Standard French and English Dictionary. Ed. J.E. Mansion. Rev. and enl. ed. by
R.P.L. Ledésert and Margaret Ledésert. 2 vols. New York: Scribner, 1973.
> Updated version with new definitions and new entries, including scientific and
technical terms with examples of usage.

The New Cassell's German Dictionary, German-English, English-German. Ed. Harold T. Bet-
teridge. Based on the editions of Karl Breul. Foreword by Gerhard Cordes. New York:
Funk & Wagnalls, 1971.
> Includes technical words and geographical and proper names. Modernized to
reflect current usage. Omits obsolete words and out-of-date material.

A New Pronouncing Dictionary of the Spanish and English Languages. Comp. Mariano Veláz-
quez de la Cadena, with Edward Gray and Juan Iribas. Rev. ed. 2 vols. in 1. New York:
Appleton/Century/Crofts, 1973.
> General purpose Spanish-English dictionary.

Taylor, James Lumpkin. A Portuguese-English Dictionary. Rev. with corrections and addi-
tions by the author and Priscilla Clark Martin. Stanford, Calif.: Stanford Univ. Press,
1970.
> Designed to provide a working language. Many technical and scientific terms
are listed, particularly names of Brazilian fauna and flora. Gives synonyms as well as
English definitions. Includes Brazilian Portuguese.

Wheeler, Marcus. The Oxford Russian-English Dictionary. Gen. ed. B.O. Unbegaun. Oxford:
Clarendon Press, 1972.
> ". . . designed primarily . . . for the use of those whose native language is
English" (Introd.). Contains colloquial terms, idioms, and some scientific words.

Special Dictionaries

Partridge, Eric. Dictionary of Slang and Unconventional English: Colloquialisms and Catch-
phrases, Solecisms and Catachreses, Nicknames, Vulgarisms, and Such Americanisms
as Have Been Naturalized. 7th ed. 2 vols. in 1. New York: Macmillan, 1970.

Roget, Peter Mark. The Original Roget's Thesaurus of English Words and Phrases. New ed.
completely revised and modernized by Robert Dutch. New York: St. Martin's Press,
1965.

Subject Dictionaries

Black, Henry Campbell. Black's Law Dictionary: Definitions of the Terms and Phrases of
American and English Jurisprudence, Ancient and Modern, with Guide to Pronuncia-

tion. 4th ed. by the publisher's editorial staff. St. Paul, Minn.: West, 1951 (Reissued 1957).

The standard dictionary for law. First edition 1891, entitled A Dictionary of Law.

Good, Carter V., ed. Dictionary of Education. 3d ed. New York: McGraw-Hill, 1973.

Definitions of words and terms in education and related fields.

Thewlis, James. Concise Dictionary of Physics and Related Subjects. Oxford: Pergamon, 1973.

". . . covers not only Physics proper, but . . . such related subjects as Astronomy, Astrophysics, Aerodynamics, Biophysics, Crystallography, Geophysics, Hydraulics, Mathematics, Medical Physics, Meteorology, Photography, Physical Chemistry, Physical Metallurgy and so on" (Foreword).

ENCYCLOPEDIAS

Encyclopedia articles give a broad survey of a topic along with descriptions and other background information. Encyclopedias are useful as a quick reference for finding information on most topics or for beginning a research project. Many encyclopedias have articles which are written and signed by specialists in their fields. The articles are frequently accompanied by bibliographies, maps, and illustrations. Most encyclopedia publishers now provide continuous revision, which means that instead of periodically releasing completely revised editions they maintain a permanent editorial staff to rework articles constantly. Each annual printing is a partial revision which attempts to keep the material up-to-date.

Articles in encyclopedias usually are arranged by either small or broad topics. In addition, many encyclopedias have an index volume useful for finding subjects not included in the alphabetical arrangement. The index of a set should be consulted first for these smaller subjects. One should also determine whether the encyclopedia is arranged alphabetically letter-by-letter or word-by-word.

General

Encyclopaedia Britannica. 15th ed. 30 vols. Chicago: Encyclopaedia Britannica, 1974. 1st-14th ed. 1768-1973.

The fifteenth edition introduces a new format in three parts and is called The New Encyclopaedia Britannica. The one-volume Propaedia, is an "Outline of Knowledge," which is a topical approach to articles in the Macropaedia. The ten-volume Micropaedia contains brief entries and serves as an index to the long articles in the Macropaedia. There are nineteen volumes in the Macropaedia which provide lengthy articles with bibliographies. Articles are signed with initials. The Propaedia gives names of contributors. The Britannica Book of the Year keeps the set up-to-date.

Encyclopedia Americana. 30 vols. New York: Encyclopedia Americana, 1975. 1st ed. 1829-1833.

> Coverage is broad with emphasis on American history, geography, and other information about the United States. Includes articles on the major literary, operatic, and theatrical masterpieces. A feature of the encyclopedia is the inclusion of the name of each century with a chronology of events of the particular century. Continuous revision. The Americana Annual summarizes events of the previous year.

Collier's Encyclopedia. 24 vols. New York: Collier, 1976. 1st ed. 1949-1951.

> Collier's is designed principally for student readership. Articles generally are less scholarly and less detailed than those in the Britannica or the Americana. The format is attractive with many excellent illustrations. Constant revision is made and articles are signed. The last volume contains a detailed index and bibliographies. Collier's is supplemented by a yearbook.

Shorter Encyclopedias

The Lincoln Library of Essential Information. Buffalo, N.Y.: Frontier Press, 1973. 1st ed. 1924.

> This work is arranged in twelve large subject areas: science, history, literature, etc. Short, unsigned articles. Each division has a subject guide, a brief bibliography, and a series of self-test questions. Continuous revision. Some editions published in two volumes.

The New Columbia Encyclopedia. 4th ed. New York: Columbia University Press, 1975. 1st ed. 1935.

> A one-volume work of some 50,000 entries; articles are brief but informative. Useful for quick reference.

Subject Encyclopedias

The Encyclopedia of Philosophy. 8 vols. New York: Macmillan, 1967.

> Includes authoritative articles covering ancient, medieval, and modern philosophy. Treats related disciplines such as mathematics, ethics, and religion. A bibliography follows each article, and there is an index at the end of volume 8.

Encyclopedia of World Art. 15 vols. New York: McGraw-Hill, 1959-1968.

> Covers every aspect of art including biographies of artists. Deals with all periods and all countries. Outstanding illustrations. Articles by specialists from many parts of the world are signed and include extensive bibliographies.

International Encyclopedia of the Social Sciences. 17 vols. New York: Macmillan, 1968.

> Lengthy, signed articles in the fields of anthropology, economics, education, geography, history, law, political science, psychology, and sociology. Scholarly articles

with bibliographies. Complements but does not supersede the Encyclopaedia of the Social Sciences.

McGraw-Hill Encyclopedia of Science and Technology; an International Reference Work. 15 vols. New York: McGraw-Hill, 1977.

Comprehensive coverage of all branches of science and technology. Designed for the layman, the articles are scholarly but not technical. Most articles are signed with initials. Extensive illustrations, many cross references, and bibliographies. Volume 15 is an index to the complete set and includes a classified topical index. Kept up-to-date by McGraw-Hill Yearbook of Science and Technology.

YEARBOOKS, ALMANACS, AND OTHER BOOKS OF FACTS AND STATISTICS

These frequently issued reference works provide current information often of a statistical nature. *Almanacs* and *other books of facts and statistics* supply many miscellaneous facts and figures on public affairs, entertainment, and notable persons as well as out-of-the-way data. *Yearbooks* usually cover events of the previous year. They may supplement encyclopedias with the latest facts and figures and are useful in historical research since the articles are written so near the time of the event. Yearbooks, almanacs, and other books of facts and statistics may be general in coverage, or they may be limited to one subject or one country.

Americana Annual, 1923 to date. New York: Encyclopedia Americana, 1923—.

Annual supplement to the Encyclopedia Americana. Universal coverage, signed articles, illustrations.

Britannica Book of the Year, 1938 to date. Chicago: Encyclopaedia Britannica, 1938—.

Annual supplement to the Encyclopaedia Britannica. Is scholarly and broad in scope. Some articles are signed with initials. A four-volume work entitled 10 Eventful Years; a Record of Events of the Years Preceding, Including and Following World War II, 1937 through 1946, summarizes the important happenings of these years.

The World Almanac and Book of Facts, 1868 to date. New York: World-Telegram, 1868—.

Miscellaneous information on population, sports, manufacturing, consumer affairs, government, and almost any topic. A special feature is a chronology of the events of the preceding year. A detailed index in the front.

Information Please Almanac, Atlas and Yearbook, 1947 to date. New York: Simon and Schuster, 1947—.

Featured topics include United States government and history, educational data, economics, and a wide range of other subjects. Articles arranged by large topics. Includes a subject index.

Statesman's Year Book; Statistical and Historical Annual of the States of the World, 1864 to
 date. London: Macmillan, 1864—.

>   Quick reference source for facts about countries of the world. Gives informa-
> tion concerning the constitution, government, economic conditions, education,
> defense, religion, courts, commerce, agriculture, and industry.

U.S. Bureau of the Census. Statistical Abstract of the United States, 1878 to date. Washington,
 D.C.: GPO, 1879—.

>   Summary of statistics gathered by the United States Government. Reports on
> the political, social, and economic aspects of the country. Gives comparative figures.

Facts on File. A Weekly Digest of World Events with Cumulative Index, 1940 to date. New
 York: Facts on File, 1940—. Loose-leaf.

>   A digest of world news with emphasis on the United States and international
> developments affecting the United States.

Keesing's Contemporary Archives; Weekly Diary of World Events with Index Continually Kept
 Up-to-date, 1931 to date. London: Keesing's, 1931—. Loose-leaf.

>   Similar to Facts on File. Good for national and international news. Includes
> texts of speeches and documents.

There are also yearbooks which are concerned with a particular country such as West
Africa Annual or with a broad subject such as Yearbook of Agriculture.

ATLASES, GAZETTEERS, AND GUIDEBOOKS

An *atlas* is a reference book designed primarily to provide maps of all kinds. Maps also
may be found in many different sources such as general encyclopedias, handbooks, almanacs,
periodicals, and newspapers. A *gazetteer* is a dictionary of geographical places usually containing no maps. In addition to geographic location, a gazetteer gives historical, cultural, statistical,
and other information about the place. *Guidebooks* also provide geographical facts. Included
are certain types of information not found in gazetteers or atlases: places of strictly local interest as well as historical significance, hotel accommodations, and other useful facts.

Adams, James Truslow, ed. Atlas of American History. New York: Scribner, 1943.

>   Geographical history of the United States arranged by date from the voyages of
> discovery to 1912. Index provides a quick reference to the maps; also serves as a cross-
> reference. Historical as well as contemporary place names are used. A supplement to
> the Dictionary of American History.

Baedeker, Karl. Baedeker's Guidebooks, 1828 to date. New York: Macmillan, 1828—.

>   Provide the traveler with useful information such as local attractions, eating
> places, and general background of the area. These guidebooks have been revised fre-
> quently. Maps are included.

Bartholomew (John) and Son, Ltd. The Times Atlas of the World: Comprehensive Edition. 2d. ed., rev. Boston: Houghton Mifflin, 1971.

> Updates the Times Atlas of the World: Mid-century Edition. Brings in new material taken from the exploration of space. Includes an index-gazetteer.

Rand McNally Commercial Atlas and Marketing Guide, 1876 to date. New York: Rand McNally, 1876—.

> An annual atlas giving business and commercial data. World coverage but emphasis on North America. The maps in this large volume supply many geographical details. This work is supplemented by the Rand McNally Road Atlas which gives road maps for the United States, Canada, and Mexico with an index to locations.

Webster's New Geographical Dictionary. Rev. ed. Springfield, Mass.: Merriam, 1972.

> Gives in alphabetical order names of places and their locations. Includes facts concerning the size, population, history, and other pertinent information on each place.

Subject Atlases

Moore, Patrick. The Atlas of the Universe. New York: Rand McNally, 1970.

The Times, London. The Times Atlas of the Moon. Ed. H.A.G. Lewis. London: Times Newspapers, Ltd., 1969.

HANDBOOKS AND MANUALS

Handbooks supply information concerning a special field, profession, or skill. Generally they are more specialized than yearbooks or almanacs and are not published annually. A *manual* is a "how-to-do" book, though not always. Sometimes they are more like handbooks.

Benét, William Rose, ed. Reader's Encyclopedia. 2d ed. New York: Crowell, 1965.

> Universal in scope. Emphasis on literature but includes music and the arts as well. Gives brief information on important literary movements, authors, literary terms and expressions, literary plots and characters, names of places and events.

Handbook of Chemistry and Physics: A Ready-reference Book of Chemical and Physical Data, 1913 to date. Cleveland, Ohio: Chemical Rubber Company, 1913—.

> Frequently updated source of information useful in the fields of chemistry, mathematics, and physics. Contains many tables and formulas.

Hart, James D. Oxford Companion to American Literature. 4th ed. New York: Oxford University Press, 1965.

> Alphabetical by author, title, and subject. Includes brief summaries of stories, poems, etc., and short biographical sketches of authors. Contains chronological index of literary and social history of America from the year 1000 to 1965.

Holman, Clarence Hugh. A Handbook to Literature. 3d ed. Based on the original by Thrall and Hibbard. Indianapolis: Odyssey Press, 1972.

> Contains an outline of British and American literary history. Discusses literary terms and concepts and schools and movements in literary history. Lists recipients of major literary prizes, such as the National Book Award, Nobel Prize, and Pulitzer Prize.

Langer, William Leonard. An Encyclopedia of World History, Ancient, Medieval, and Modern; Chronologically Arranged. 5th ed. rev. and enl. Boston: Houghton Mifflin, 1972.

> A one-volume record of the world's history from prehistoric times to 1970. Good for comparative purposes. Includes some historical maps and genealogy tables of ruling dynasties.

Political Handbook and Atlas of the World; Parliaments, Parties and Press . . . , 1927 to date. New York: Harper and Row, 1927—.

> Handbook describing the governments of the world and their leaders. Issued annually. Maps added in 1963. Supplemented by The World This Year.

Robert, Henry M. Robert's Rules of Order Newly Revised. New and enl. by Sarah Corbin Robert. Chicago: Scott, Foresman, 1970.

> The standard parliamentary guide since 1876 for the conduct of business meetings of large organizations. The new edition contains a quick reference section on different types of procedures and their usage.

Turabian, Kate L. A Manual for Writers of Term Papers, Theses, and Dissertations. 4th ed. Chicago: University of Chicago Press, 1973.

> Handy guide for information on bibliographic forms, footnotes, and the mechanics of writing research papers.

United States Government Manual, 1935 to date. Washington, D.C.: GPO, 1935—.

> Issued annually and is the official handbook on the workings of the United States government. Describes the agencies of all three branches plus certain semiofficial agencies. Contains a copy of the United States Constitution and a list of abbreviations of government agency names.

BIOGRAPHICAL DICTIONARIES

Information about people frequently is needed for a paper, speech, or other research. Particularly outstanding people are included in many different kinds of *biographical dictionaries*—those that are universal in scope such as *Current Biography;* those limited geographically such as *Who's Who in America;* or ones limited to a particular profession or skill such as *American Men and Women of Science.* Some figures in history are less outstanding than others and may be included only in one kind of biographical dictionary. In seeking information, the researcher should consider three questions: What is the nationality of the person? Is he living or no longer living? What is his profession? Sometimes the student knows little or nothing about the individual. To find answers to these questions, the researcher should consider the following procedure:

1. *What is the nationality of the individual?*

The card catalog is a source which might give this information. A book by the person or about him probably would indicate the place of publication. Possibly the birth date or death date might appear on the catalog card. The subject card would tell the field of interest and in some cases the location of his research project. Other information, such as the position he holds, the organization with which he is affiliated, or the university in which he teaches, may appear on the title page of a book written by him.

The *Biography Index* could be consulted. This source includes the nationality, dates, and the profession of the person named.

Trade bibliographies, usually limited to the book production of a particular country, may provide the information. *Cumulative Book Index* is a guide to books written in the English language with author, title, and subject approaches. Other trade bibliographies to consider are: *British Books in Print, Bibliographie de la France, Brinkman's Cumulative Catalogus Van Boeken, Deutsche Bibliographie,* to name a few.

Periodical indexes could be checked for articles by or about a person. Newspaper indexes sometimes include names of individuals who may appear in the news only once.

2. *Is the person living or dead?*

After the nationality of a person has been established, the doors are open to find biographical sources for either the living or non-living. *Who's Who* of almost any country will give information on living persons. Several sources which provide brief information about persons of all times and places are: *Webster's Biographical Dictionary, The New Century Cyclopedia of Names,* and *Universal Pronouncing Dictionary of Biography and Mythology.* To locate persons currently in the news, one should consult *Current Biography* or *International Who's Who.*

For people no longer living, the *Dictionary of American Biography* and *Dictionary of National Biography* for Americans and British, respectively, give lengthy, signed articles with bibliographies. Here again the card catalog, *Biography Index,* and trade bibliographies may be consulted.

3. *What is the profession of the individual?*

Sometimes a person may be known only in the field in which he works rather than on a national basis. Examples of sources of information by profession are: *Who's Who in American Education, World Who's Who in Finance and Industry, Who's Who in the Theatre, Who's Who in American Art, Who's Who in American Politics,* and many others.

Universal (General)

New Century Cyclopedia of Names. Ed. C.L. Barnhart with the assistance of William D. Halsey and others. 3 vols. New York: Appleton, 1954.

> Brief articles. Includes people, places, historical events, characters in literature, works of art, legendary persons, and places. Pronunciations are given as well as descriptions. Also contains a short chronology of world history and genealogy charts.

Webster's Biographical Dictionary. Springfield, Mass.: Merriam, 1974.

> Brief biographical sketches of noteworthy persons of all periods in history and of all occupations. Universal in scope.

Universal (Living)

Current Biography, 1940 to date. New York: H. W. Wilson, 1940—.

> Lengthy, informative sketches of people in the news. Universal in coverage, including many fields such as politics, the theatre, sports, etc. Portrait is included for each person as well as a bibliography. Necrologies and a cumulative index are other features. Monthly with yearly cumulations. Index in the 1950 annual covers the years 1940-1950; 1960 volume covers 1951 through 1960. Since the latter date, each annual has cumulated the indexes of all years since 1960.

International Who's Who, 1935 to date. London: Europa Publications and Allen & Unwin, 1935—.

> Published annually, universal in scope, short articles of prominent men and women. Includes obituary section listing those who have died since the preceding volume was published.

National (Deceased)

Dictionary of American Biography. Published under the auspices of the American Council of Learned Societies. 20 vols. and index. New York: Scribner, 1928-1937. Supplements 1-4, 1944-1974.

> Included in this scholarly dictionary, frequently referred to as the DAB, are notable Americans who are no longer living. Lengthy articles are signed and include excellent bibliographies. No illustrations. Prominent people in many areas are included. Supplements bring the dictionary up-to-date through 1950.

Dictionary of National Biography. Ed. Sir Leslie Stephen and Sir Sidney Lee. 22 vols. London: Smith, Elder, 1908-1909. Supplements 2d-7th. London: 0xford University Press, 1912-1971.

> Often referred to as the DNB, this is the national biography for Great Britain. Includes Americans of the Colonial period. Long, scholarly articles are signed and include bibliographies. Supplements bring the dictionary up-to-date through 1960.

Who Was Who in America. A Companion Biographical Reference Work to Who's Who in America, 1897-1973. Chicago: Marquis, 1942-1973.

> The American counterpart of Who Was Who includes biographies of Americans no longer living who were once included in Who's Who in America. The volume covering 1969-1973 is a cumulative index to all volumes of Who Was Who in America.

National (Living)

Who's Who, an Annual Biographical Dictionary . . . , 1849 to date. London: Black, 1849—.

> Concise, unsigned biographical sketches of notable living Englishmen. Includes some prominent international figures.

Who's Who in America, 1899/1900 to date. Chicago: Marquis, 1899—.

> Short, unsigned biographies of living Americans and some non-Americans prominent in this country. Name cross references to other Marquis publications such as Who's Who in the South and Southwest, Who's Who in the West, and others.

Special Fields

Literature

Twentieth Century Authors. Ed. Stanley J. Kunitz and Howard Haycraft. New York: H.W. Wilson, 1942. First Supplement. Ed. Stanley J. Kunitz and Vineta Colby, 1955.

> Gives authors of this century with a list of their works. Universal in scope. Portraits and bibliographies included. Supplement adds 700 new authors.

World Authors, 1950-1970. Ed. John Wakeman. New York: H.W. Wilson, 1975.

> Designed to accompany Twentieth Century Authors. This work adds over 900 new authors.

Science

American Men and Women of Science. 12th ed. New York: Jaques Cattell Press/Bowker, 1971—.

> Issued in two sections—Physical and Biological Sciences, 6 vols., and Social and Behavioral Sciences, 2 vols. Short sketches listing personal data, accomplishments, and publications. Frequent revisions.

DIRECTORIES

Directories list the names and addresses of persons, organizations, or institutions. Other information about organizations such as purposes, dues, and officers are often included. Oftentimes the value of a directory may be overlooked. Names of executives may be found in a directory and nowhere else. Sometimes old directories may provide valuable historical information.

U.S. Congress. <u>Official Congressional Directory for the Use of the United States Congress</u>, 1809 to date. Washington, D.C.: GPO, 1809—.

> Called the <u>Congressional Directory</u>. Gives names, addresses, and biographical sketches of members of Congress. Also includes names and addresses of top officials of all the agencies, committees, etc. Maps showing congressional districts.

<u>Encyclopedia of Associations</u>. 12th ed. 3 vols. Detroit: Gale, 1978.

> Volume 1, <u>National Organizations of the United States</u>—descriptions of active organizations and lists of non-functioning groups. Arranged in subject areas. Volume 2, <u>Geographic and Executive Index</u>—a list of entries by state and city and a list of executives. Volume 3, <u>New Associations and Projects</u>—gives the same information found in volume 1 for new organizations.

<u>Thomas' Register of American Manufacturers</u>, 1905 to date. New York: Thomas Publishing Company, 1905—.

> Published annually. This work gives major American companies and their products, services, personnel, and ratings. Listed by products and services, by company names, and by brand names.

Scholars

<u>Directory of American Scholars, a Biographical Directory</u>. 6th ed. 4 vols. New York: Bowker, 1974.

> Similar to <u>American Men and Women of Science</u> with emphasis on humanities, education, law, and history. Has cross references to <u>American Men and Women of Science</u>.

Statesmen

U.S. Congress. <u>Biographical Directory of the American Congress, 1774-1971</u>. Washington, D.C.: GPO, 1971.

> Short biographical sketches of the Senators and Representatives from each state, starting with the Continental Congress and continuing through each Congress to the 91st. Also lists executive officers and cabinet members.

BIBLIOGRAPHIES

Bibliographies are lists of sources of information—books, periodicals, films, and the like. Their value as a research tool is obvious. There are many bibliographies—some devoted to one subject and some general in nature. Only two will be mentioned here.

<u>The Bibliographic Index; a Cumulative Bibliography of Bibliographies</u>, 1937 to date. New York: H.W. Wilson, 1938—.

> A subject list of bibliographies that have appeared in books and magazines as well as those that have been published as separates. Issued twice a year and cumulates

annually. Some of the bibliographies are annotated; others only give author, title, and publication information.

Cumulative Book Index, a World List of Books in the English Language, 1928/32 to date. New York: H.W. Wilson, 1933—.

      Originally published as a supplement to the United States Catalog (1898-1928). Lists books published in the United States and Canada and selected publications from other English-speaking countries. Arranged by author, title, and subject in dictionary fashion.

CONCORDANCES

    A *concordance* is an alphabetical list of words or phrases found in a work or the works of one author and gives the context in which each word or phrase appears.

Bartlett, John. New and Complete Concordance or Verbal Index to Words, Phrases, and Passages in the Dramatic Works of Shakespeare, with a Supplementary Concordance to the Poems. London: Macmillan, 1894.

      Gives the full context in which each word is used along with its location—act, scene, and line. The numbers refer to the Globe edition, 1891.

Nelson's Complete Concordance of the Revised Standard Version Bible. Comp. John Ellison. New York: Nelson, 1957.

      Computer listing of key words in the Bible with context and location of each word.

INDEXES AND ABSTRACTS

    Indexes and *abstracts* are types of reference books which point to information in other sources. These will be considered in another chapter.

SELECTED SUBJECT REFERENCE BOOKS

Agriculture and Home Economics

Almanac of the Canning, Freezing and Preserving Industry. 1916—.
Diseases and Pests of Ornamental Plants. 4th ed. 1970.
Encyclopedia of Food Technology. 1974.
Exotic Plant Manual: Fascinating Plants to Live with—Their Requirements, Propagation and Use. 1970.
Forestry Handbook. 1955.
Handbook of Food Additives. 1968.
Wyman's Gardening Encyclopedia. 1971.
Yearbook of Agriculture. 1894—.

Anthropology and Ethnology

The American Negro Reference Book. 1966.
Dictionary of Anthropology. 1964.
Handbook of American Indians: North of Mexico. 2 vols. 1971.
A Handbook of Method in Cultural Anthropology. 1970.
Handbook of Middle American Indians. 12 vols. (In progress, to be in 16 vols.) 1964-1972.
Handbook of Social and Cultural Anthropology. 1973.
Handbook of South American Indians. 7 vols. 1946-1959.
A Hundred Years of Anthropology. 1952.
The Origin of Races. 1962.
The Student Anthropologist's Handbook: A Guide to Research, Training and Career. 1972.

Archaeology

The Concise Encyclopedia of Archaeology. 2d ed. 1971.
Larousse Encyclopedia of Archaeology. 1972.

Art

The Britannica Encyclopaedia of American Art. 1974.
Dictionary of Design and Decoration. 1973.
Encyclopedia of Modern Architecture. 1963.
Encyclopedia of Urban Planning. 1974.
Encyclopedia of World Art. 15 vols. 1959-1968.
A History of Architecture on the Comparative Method for Students, Craftsmen and Amateurs. 1961.
History of Art: A Survey of the Major Visual Arts from the Dawn of History to the Present Day. 1969.
Pelican History of Art. 38 vols. (In progress to be completed in 50 vols.) 1953-1974.

Astronomy

The Concise Atlas of the Universe. 1974.
A New Photographic Atlas of the Moon. 1971.
The Telescope Handbook and Star Atlas. 1975.
The Times Atlas of the Moon. 1969.

Biology

A Dictionary of Genetics. 2d ed. rev. 1974.
The Encyclopedia of Microscopy and Microtechnique. 1973.
The Encyclopedia of the Biological Sciences. 2d ed. 1970.

Botany

A Dictionary of Flowering Plants and Ferns. 8th ed. 1973.
A Dictionary of Useful and Everyday Plants and Their Common Names. 1974.
A Guide to the Medicinal Plants of the United States. 1973.
Wildflowers of the United States. 6 vols. plus index. 1966-1975.

Business

Dictionary of Accountants. 5th ed. 1975.
Dictionary of Economic Terms. 1970.
Dictionary of Economics. 5th ed. 1971.
Economics 73/74 Encyclopedia. 1973.
Encyclopedia of Auditing Techniques. 2 vols. 1967.
Encyclopedia of Banking and Finance. 7th ed. 1973.
Encyclopedia of Management. 2d ed. 1973.
Insurance Almanac. 1913—.
McGraw-Hill Dictionary of Modern Economics; a Handbook of Terms and Organizations. 2d
    ed. 1973.
Statistical Abstract of the United States. 1879—.
Thomas' Register of American Manufacturers. 1905—.

Chemistry and Physics

The Chemist's Companion: A Handbook of Practical Data, Techniques and References. 1972.
Concise Dictionary of Physics and Related Subjects. 1973.
The Encyclopedia of Chemistry. 3d ed. 1973.
Encyclopedia of Electrochemistry of the Elements. 1 vol. (15 volumes estimated by the
    publisher). 1973.
Encyclopedia of Physics. 2d ed. 1974.
Handbook of Chemistry and Physics. 1974.
Lange's Handbook of Chemistry. 11th ed. 1973.

Earth Sciences

A Dictionary of Geology. 4th ed. 1974.
The Encyclopedia of Geochemistry and Environmental Sciences. Vol. 4 A of *Encyclopedia of
    Earth Sciences.* 1972.
Encyclopedia of Minerals. 1974.
The Water Encyclopedia: A Compendium of Useful Information on Water Resources. 1970.
The Weather Almanac. 1974.

Education

Career Guidance: A Handbook of Methods. 1973.
Dictionary of Education. 3d ed. 1973.
Education in the States. 2 vols. 1969.
Education Yearbook. 1972—.
Encyclopedia of Careers and Vocational Guidance. 2 vols. 1972.
Encyclopedia of Education. 10 vols. 1971.
Encyclopedia of Educational Evaluation. 1975.
Encyclopedia of Educational Research. 4th ed. 1969.
Handbook of Adult Education. 1970.
International Encyclopedia of Higher Education. 10 vols. 1977.
Occupational Education. 1971.

Technician Education Yearbook. 1963.
The World Year Book of Education. 1931—.
Yearbook of Special Education. 1975.

Engineering and Technology

Airplanes: From the Dawn of Flight to the Present Day. 1973.
Chemical and Process Technology Encyclopedia. 1974.
The Complete Encyclopedia of Motor Cars 1885-1960. 1969.
Computer Dictionary and Handbook. 2d ed. 1972.
Dictionary of Architecture and Construction. 1975.
A Dictionary of Building. 2d ed. 1974.
A Dictionary of Computers. 1970.
Elsevier's Dictionary of Chemical Engineering. 2 vols. 1969.
Encyclopedia of Computer Science and Technology. 1 vol. (In progress, to be completed in 15 vols.) 1975.
Encyclopedia of Instrumentation and Controls. 1972.
Encyclopedia of Space Science. 1963.
Engineering Encyclopedia. 1963.
McGraw-Hill Encyclopedia of Energy. 1976.
Motor's Auto Repair Manual. 1976.
Railroads. 1975.
Standard Handbook of Engineering Calculations. 1972.
The Way Things Work Book of the Computer: An Illustrated Encyclopedia of Information Science, Cybernetics, and Data Processing. 1974.

Environmental Sciences

Dictionary of Environmental Sciences. 1973.
Handbook of Environmental Control. 1972.
Handbook of Water Resources and Pollution Control. 1976.
McGraw-Hill Encyclopedia of Environmental Science. 1974.
The New York Times Encyclopedic Dictionary of the Environment, 1971.
Water and Water Pollution Handbook. 4 vols. 1971.

Geography

Larousse Encyclopedia of World Geography. 1965.
Dictionary of Geography (Monkhouse). 1970.

History

Album of American History. 6 vols. 1969.
Chronological History of the Negro in America. 1969.
Documents of American History. 9th ed. 1973.
Encyclopedia of American History. 3d ed. 1970.
Encyclopedia of Latin America. 1974.
The Encyclopedia of Military History. 1970.

Encyclopedia of the American Revolution. 1974.
An Encyclopedia of World History, Ancient, Medieval and Modern; Chronologically Arranged. 5th ed. rev. 1972.
Historical Statistics of the United States, Colonial Times to 1970. 2 vols. 1975.

Journalism

The Dartnell Advertising Manager's Handbook. 1969.
Encyclopedia of Advertising. 1969.
Handbook of Advertising Management. 1970.
Printing and Promotion Handbook: How to Plan, Produce and Use Printing, Advertising and Direct Mail. 1966.
The Writer's Handbook. 1975.

Law

Black's Law Dictionary. 4th ed. 1957.
Encyclopedic Dictionary of Business Law. 1961.
The Environmental Law Handbook. 1971.
Handbook of Federal Narcotic and Dangerous Drug Laws. 1969.
Handbook on Consumer Law. 1968.
The Medical Sourcebook. 1959.
Women's Rights Almanac. 1974.

Literature

General

Cassell's Encyclopedia of World Literature. 3 vols. 1973.
Contemporary Literary Criticism. 1973 to date. 8 vols. 1973—.
Encyclopedia of Mystery and Detection. 1976.
Encyclopedia of Science Fiction and Fantasy. 2 vols. 1974.
Encyclopedia of World Literature in the 20th Century. 3 vols. 1967-71. Vol. 4, *Supplement* and *Index.* 1975.
Familiar Quotations (Bartlett's). 14th ed. rev. & enl. 1968.
A Handbook of Literature. Based on the original by Thrall and Hibbard. 3d ed. 1972.
The International Thesaurus of Quotations. 1970.
A Library of Literary Criticism: Modern Latin American Literature. 1975.
Literary Terms: A Dictionary. 1975.
The Penguin Companion to World Literature. 4 vols. 1969-1971.
Poetry Handbook. 1974.
Princeton Encyclopedia of Poetry and Poetics. 1975.
The Reader's Encyclopedia. 2d ed. 1965.
Twentieth Century Writing: A Reader's Guide to Contemporary Literature. 1969.
World Encyclopedia of Comics. 1976.

American Literature

Cambridge History of American Literature. 4 vols. 1917-1921.
Crowell's Handbook of Contemporary American Poetry: A Critical Handbook of American Poetry Since 1940. 1974.
Library of Literary Criticism of English and American Authors. 4 vols. 1966.
Literary History of the United States (Spiller's). 4th ed. rev. 2 vols. 1974.
Oxford Companion to American Literature. 1965.
The Penguin Companion to American Literature. 1971.

English Literature

Cambridge History of English Literature. 15 vols. 1907-33.
The Concise Encyclopedia of English and American Poets and Poetry. 1963.
Concise Oxford Dictionary of English Literature. 1970.
A Library of Literary Criticism: Modern British Literature. 3 vols. 1966.
New Century Handbook of English Literature. 1967.
The Penguin Companion to English Literature. 1971.

Mathematics

Handbook of Applied Mathematics. 1966.
Handbook of Mathematical Tables and Formulas. 5th ed. 1973.
Mathematical Handbook for Scientists and Engineers; Definitions, Theorems, and Formulas for Reference and Review. 1968.
The Universal Encyclopedia of Mathematics. 1964.

Medical Sciences

Black's Medical Dictionary. 30th ed. 1974.
Blakiston Gould Medical Dictionary. 3d ed. 1972.
Current Therapy. Latest Approved Methods of Treatment for the Practicising Physician. 1949—.
Cyclopedia of Medicine, Surgery, Specialties. 15 vols. 1950—.
Dictionary of Medical Syndromes. 1971.
Drugs in Current Use and New Drugs. 1955—.
Encyclopedia of Animal Care. 10th ed. 1972.
Encyclopedia of Sport Sciences and Medicine. 1971.
Handbook for the Orthopedic Assistant. 1976.
Handbook of Diet Therapy. 1970.
Handbook of Speech Pathology and Audiology. 1971.
Handbook of Vitamins and Hormones. 1973.
Merck Manual of Diagnosis and Therapy. 13th ed. 1977.
Stedman's Medical Dictionary. 22d ed. 1972.

Military Science

The Almanac of World Military Power. 3d ed. 1974.
Dictionary of Battles. Rev. ed. 1971.
Dictionary of Weapons and Military Terms. 1973.

Motion Pictures, Radio, and Television

Alphabetical Guide to Motion Picture, Television and Videotape Production. 1970.
Broadcasting Yearbook. 1935—.
Film Facts. 1938—.
The Filmgoer's Companion. 4th ed. 1974.
The Focal Encyclopedia of Film and Television Techniques. 1969.
International Motion Picture Almanac. 1929—.
The American Movies Reference Book: The Sound Era. 1969.

Music

Baker's Biographical Dictionary of Musicians. 6th ed. c 1978.
Dictionary of Contemporary Music. 1974.
Dictionary of Music and Musicians (Grove's). 5th ed. 9 vols. 1954. *Supplement.* 1961.
The Encyclopedia of Jazz. 1960.
Harvard Dictionary of Music. 2nd ed. 1969.
Illustrated Encyclopedia of Rock. 1977
The Oxford Companion to Music. 10th ed. 1970.
The World of Musical Comedy: The Story of the American Musical Stage as Told Through the Careers of Its Foremost Composers and Lyricists. 1969.

Mythology and Folklore

Brewer's Dictionary of Phrase and Fable. Centenary ed. 1970.
Crowell's Handbook of Classical Mythology. 1970.
Encyclopedia of Superstitions. 1961.
Encyclopedia of Witchcraft and Demonology. 1959.
The Golden Bough: A Study in Magic and Religion. 13 vols. 1955.
Man, Myth, and Magic. 24 vols. 1970.
The New Century Handbook of Greek Mythology and Legend. 1972.

Philosophy

Dictionary of the History of Ideas: Studies of Selected Pivotal Ideas. 5 vols. 1973-74.
The Encyclopedia of Philosophy. 8 vols. 1967.

Political Science

A Dictionary of Politics. Rev. ed. 1974.
History of American Presidential Elections 1789-1968. 4 vols. 1971.
The International Relations Dictionary. 1969.
Marxism, Communism and Western Society: A Comparative Encyclopedia. 8 vols. 1972-1973.
National Party Platforms: 1840-1972. 5th ed. 1973.
Political Handbook and Atlas of the World. 1927—.
Statesman's Year Book. 1864—.
United States Government Manual. 1935—.
World Communism: A Handbook 1918-1965. 1973.
Worldmark Encyclopedia of the Nations. 5 vols. 1971.

Psychology

Dictionary of Behavioral Science. 1974.
The Encyclopedia of Human Behavior; Psychology, Psychiatry, and Mental Health. 2 vols.
    1970.
Encyclopedia of Mental Health. 6 vols. 1963.
Encyclopedia of Psychology. 3 vols. 1972.
Mental Measurements Yearbook. 1938—.
The New Encyclopedia of Child Care and Guidance. Rev. ed. 1971.

Recreation and Sports

Encyclopedia of Sports. 4th rev. ed. 1969.
Sportsman's Encyclopedia. 1971.

Religion

Dictionary of Comparative Religion. 1970.
Encyclopaedia Judaica. 16 vols. 1972.
Encyclopaedia of Religion and Ethics. 13 vols. 1908-1927.
New Catholic Encyclopedia. 15 vols. 1967.
New Schaff-Herzog Encyclopedia of Religious Knowledge. 13 vols. 1949-1950.

Science—General

Britannica Yearbook of Science and the Future. 1968—.
Harper Encyclopedia of Science. Rev. ed. 1967.
McGraw-Hill Encyclopedia of Science and Technology. 15 vols. 1977.
McGraw-Hill Yearbook of Science and Technology. 1962—.
Science Year: The World Book Science Annual. 1965—.
Van Nostrand's Scientific Encyclopedia. 5th ed. 1976.

Social Sciences—General

A Dictionary of the Social Sciences. 1964.
Encyclopaedia of the Social Sciences. 15 vols. 1930-1935.
International Encyclopedia of the Social Sciences. 17 vols. 1968.

Sociology and Social Work

*Bloodletters and Badmen: A Narrative Encyclopedia of American Criminals from the Pilgrims
    to the Present*. 1973.
Dictionary of Modern Sociology. 1969.
Encyclopedia of Social Work. 1965.
Encyclopedia of Sociology. 1974.

Speech

Handbook for Discussion Leaders. Rev. ed. 1954.
Representative American Speeches. 1937/38—.
Robert's Rules of Order Newly Revised. 1970.

Textiles

AF Encyclopedia of Textiles. 2d ed. 1972.
American Cotton Handbook. 2d rev. ed. 1949.
Fabric Almanac. 2d ed. 1971.
The Standard Handbook of Textiles. 8th ed. 1975.
Textile Handbook. 4th ed. 1970.
Wool Handbook. 3d enl. ed. 2 vols. in 3. 1963-1970.

Theater

Best Plays and the Yearbook of the Drama in America. 1926—.
Crowell's Handbook of Contemporary Drama. 1971.
McGraw-Hill Encyclopedia of World Drama. 4 vols. 1972.
Plays, Players, and Playwrights: An Illustrated History of the Theatre. 1971.
The Reader's Encyclopedia of World Drama. 1969.
Stage Management and Theatrecraft: A Stage Manager's Handbook. 1968.

Zoology

American Seashells: The Marine Mollusca of the Atlantic & Pacific Coast of North America. 2d ed. 1974.
Birds of the World: A Check List. 1973.
The Dictionary of Butterflies & Moths in Color. 1975.
The Dinosaur Dictionary. 1972.
Fishes of the World: An Illustrated Dictionary. 1975.
Grzimek's Animal Life Encyclopedia. 13 vols. 1972-1975.
The Illustrated Encyclopedia of the Animal Kingdom. 2d English ed. 20 vols. 1972.
Insects of the World. 1972.
The International Wildlife Encyclopedia. 20 vols. 1969-1970.
Larousse Encyclopedia of Animal Life. 1967.
Mammals of the World. Rev. for 3d ed. 2 vols. 1975.
The New Field Book of Reptiles and Amphibians. 1970.

7
INDEXES

The library catalog usually does not provide direct access to articles in periodicals, newspapers, or books. Indexes of various types provide the key to locating this kind of material. Library collections usually include a variety of indexes which cite exact references to items included in periodicals, newspapers, and anthologies.

The following types of indexes will be discussed in this chapter with representative titles in each group:

1. Periodical indexes and abstracts.
2. Newspaper indexes.
3. Indexes to book reviews.
4. Indexes to literature appearing in anthologies or collections.
5. Indexes to literary criticism.

PERIODICAL INDEXES AND ABSTRACTS

Periodical indexes provide the information needed to locate articles appearing in thousands of magazines and journals. Some of the indexes, such as *The Readers' Guide to Periodical Literature,* are general in coverage; that is, they include many subjects and index, for the most part, popular magazines. Other indexes deal principally with one subject area and index journals with scholarly articles, for example, *Applied Science and Technology Index.* Generally, each index includes different magazines and journals although there are some which overlap.

Periodical literature is valuable as a research medium for a number of reasons. The material found in magazines, journals, and newspapers is the most recent information one can find. By locating an article written shortly after an event occurred, whether it be in the 19th century, the 1930's, or whatever, the library user will find contemporary opinion which reflects what people thought of the event at the time it occurred. It is also possible to find comparative information for different periods. Sometimes periodical literature is the only information available—the topic may be too faddish ever to appear in a book. The findings of researchers and scholars are published in professional journals which supplement other types of literature in a particular field, such as medicine or education. There are times when a book or selections from books appear in magazines and journals before they are published in their final form.

Most of the periodical indexes issue monthly copies and at the end of the year publish an annual cumulation in which all of the articles included in the magazines and journals indexed by a particular service are arranged in one alphabet.

General

Readers' Guide to Periodical Literature, 1900 to date. New York: H.W. Wilson, 1900—.

<u>Readers' Guide</u> is probably the most widely used and well-known of all the periodical indexes. It originally indexed about fifteen of the most popular magazines and now indexes more than 175 different periodicals. The magazines indexed are general in nature, covering all subject areas. Knowing how to use <u>Readers' Guide</u> enables one to use other indexes more efficiently. Its arrangement and use are explained in detail below.

Frequency

Readers' Guide is published twice a month except February, July, and August when it appears monthly. The materials in the first issue of each month are cumulated (included in one alphabet) in the second issue of each month. The monthly issues cumulate every three months. The paperbound issues are replaced by a cumulative bound volume at the end of the year.

Arrangement

Each issue of *Readers' Guide* is divided into several important sections. These are: (1) a list of abbreviations of periodicals indexed with the explanation of the abbreviations, (2) a list of the periodicals indexed, (3) a list of other abbreviations used in the index, (4) the main body of the index consisting of subject and author entries, and (5) a listing of book reviews by authors with citations. Earlier issues of *Readers' Guide* included book reviews in the main body of the entries under the author's name.

Articles are listed alphabetically by subject and author. Title entries for dramas, operas, and ballets are treated as cross references. Entries from *Readers' Guide* are shown below.

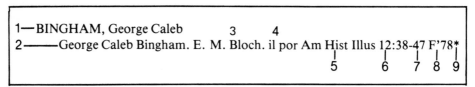

Figure 7-1. Subject entry.

1. Subject heading (on a line by itself in bold face type).
2. Title of article.
3. Author's last name and initials.
4. Descriptive information—illustration and portrait.
5. Abbreviated name of the magazine in which the article appears.
6. Volume number.
7. Inclusive paging.
8. Date of the magazine (abbreviated).
9. Asterisk indicates that "Bingham, George Caleb" is used here as a subject and not as an author.

> BLOCH, E. Maurice
> George Caleb Bingham. il por Am Hist Illus 12:38-47 F '78

Figure 7-2. Author entry.

In an author entry, the author's full name appears first in heavy print on a line by itself. The author entries contain the same information as the subject entries except that the author's name is not repeated after the title.

Readers' Guide does not list articles by title although titles of plays, operas, and ballets are used as cross references. In older issues, cross references were included for titles of short stories. Plays are listed under the subject heading "Dramas—Criticisms, plots, etc." as well as by author and title. Reviews of movies are listed under the subject heading "Motion picture reviews." In the older indexes, movie reviews were listed under the subject heading "Moving picture plays—Criticisms, plots, etc." Poems are listed by author only, but in older issues of the indexes they are listed by title.

The indexes contain many *see* and *see also* references which direct the reader to other names and subjects. A *see* reference refers the reader from a name, subject, or title that is not used to one that is used. A *see also* reference refers the reader to additional subject headings.

How to locate an article

If the researcher wishes to locate an article he has found in the index, he should:

1. Copy accurately all information about the article: author, title of article, full title of periodical (consult list of abbreviations to get full name of periodical), volume number, date, and inclusive pages.

2. Locate the periodical. Procedures for finding periodicals vary in libraries. Follow the procedures of the particular library for locating the periodical. These are often explained in the library handbook.

Poole's Index to Periodical Literature 1802-1907. 7 vols. Boston: Houghton, 1882-1908.

Poole's is a subject index to approximately 475 American and English magazines published during the 1800's. Entries include all information for locating the article except the date. Periodicals are listed alphabetically in the front with a chronological conspectus number which leads the reader by means of a table to the date.

British Humanities Index, 1962 to date. London: Library Association, 1963—.

Indexes materials relating to subjects such as politics, economics, history, and literature in 380 British periodicals. Published quarterly with annual cumulations.

Canadian Periodical Index, 1964 to date. Ottawa: Canadian Library Association, 1964—.

Author and subject index to a wide variety of Canadian periodicals. An earlier version published by the Ontario Department of Education covered the years 1928-1947. From 1948-1963 the title changed to Canadian Index to Periodicals and Documentary Films. Now published monthly with annual cumulations.

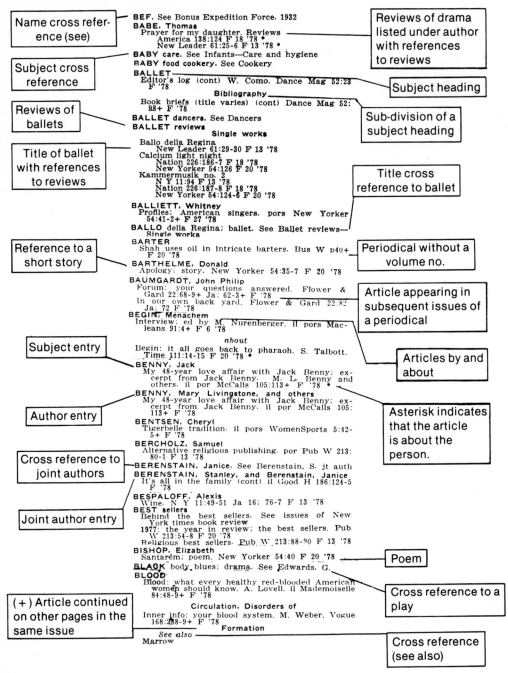

Figure 7-3. Selected references from *Readers' Guide to Periodical Literature.*

Adams, A. Listening to Billie
  N Y Times Bk R 83:15+ F 26 '78. J. L. Crain
Aitchison, J. Articulate mammal: an introduction
  to psycholinguistics
  Sci Am 238:44-5 F '78. P. Morrison
Alexander, H. To covet honor: a biography of
  Alexander Hamilton
  Nat R 30:227 F 17 '78. A. Bakshian, jr
Aleyev, Y. G. Nekton. 1977
  Science 199:678 F 10 '78. P. W. Webb
Arendt, H. Life of the mind, v 1: Thinking; v2:
  Willing
  New Repub 178:47-8 F 25 '78. J. M. Altman
Arens, R. ed. Genocide in Paraguay; epilogue by
  E. Wiesel
  Nation 226:181-3 F 18 '78. I. L. Horowitz
Armstrong, G. Wanderers all: an American pil-
  grimage
  Blair & Ketchums 5:87-9 F '78. L. P. Hunting-
  ton

Bainbridge, B. Injury time
  N Y Times Bk R 83:15 F 26 '78. K. Pollitt
Barke, P. G. Potential scattering in atomc phys-
  ics. 1977
  Science 199:677 F 10 '78. A. Temkin
Bataille, G. Story of the eye; tr. by J. Neugro-
  schel
  N Y Times Bk R 83:13 F 12 '78. P. Brooks
Bate, W. J. Samuel Johnson
  N Y Times Bk R 83:3+ F 26 '78. R. Locke
Beckett, S. Collected poems in English and French
  New Repub 178:33-5 F 18 '78. E. Brater
Benson, E. F. Make way for Lucia
  America 138:125-6 F 18 '78. P. Matthews
Bercovitch, R. Hasen
  N Y Times Bk R 83:12+ F 12 '78. A. Broyard
Berleth, R. Twilight lords: an Irish chronicle
  New Repub 178:37-8 F 18 '78. R. Stilling
Berlin, I. Vico and Herder: two studies in the
  history of ideas
  America 138:152-6 F 25 '78. J. Gustaitis
Berrone, L. James Joyce in Padua
  New Repub 178:28-31 F 18 '78. N. Montgomery
Berry, W. Unsettling of America: culture and
  agriculture
  Progressive 42:43-4 F '78. S. Sanders
Bethge, E. Bonhoeffer: exile and martyr
  Commonweal 105:124-6 F 17 '78. M. F. Mc-
  Cauley
Bird, R. B. and others. Dynamics of polymeric
  liquids. 2v. 1977
  Phys Today 31:54-7 F '78. S. Middleman
Blair, T. L. Retreat to the ghetto
  New Leader 61:21-2 F 13 '78. G. Gilder
Boldrey, R. and Boldrey, J. Chauvinist or fem-
  inist? Paul's view of women. 1976
  Chr Today 22:40-2 F 10 '78. P. Siddons
Böll, H. Heinrich Böll: Missing persons and other
  essays; tr. by L. Vennewitz
  America 138:151-2 F 25 '78. D. Coogan
Borzoi anthology of Latin American literature; ed.
  by E. Rodriguez Monegal; with T. Colchie. 2v.
  1977
  Américas 30:26-8 F '78. M. Gowland de Gallo
Bosworth, P. Montgomery Clift
  Newsweek 91:76 F 27 '78. J. N. Baker
Braginsky, V. B. and Manukin, A. B. Measure-
  ment of weak forces in physics experiments.
  1977
  Phys Today 31:51-2 F '78. W. O. Hamilton
Bronowski, J. Sense of the future: essays in natu-
  ral philosophy
  N Y Times Bk R 83:10+ F 12 '78. G. Jonas
Bronson, W. Last grand adventure; with R. Rein-
  hardt. 1977
  Sunset 160:23 F '78
Brooks, T. R. Communications Workers of Amer-
  ica
  Wash M 9:63-4 F '78. R. Reeves
Bruch, H. Golden cage: the enigma of anorexia
  nervosa
  Psychol Today 11:118-19+ F '78. M. Scarf
Bull, J. and Farrand, J. jr. Audubon society field
  guide to North American birds: eastern region
  Natur Hist 87:98+ F '78. M. Harwood
Burchard, J. Bernini is dear? Architecture and
  the social purpose. 1976

Caplan, F. and Caplan, T. Second twelve months
  of life: a kaleidosocpe of growth
  N Y Times Bk R 83:9+ F 12 '78. E. L. White
Chang, K. C. ed. Food in Chinese culture: an-
  thropoligcal and historical perspectives
  Sci Am 238:34+ F '78. P. Morrison
Charles-Dominique, P. Ecology and behaviour of
  nocturnal primates: prosimians of Equatorial
  West Africa; tr. by R. D. Martin
  Sci Am 238:40+ F '78. P. Morrison
Cheek, L. M. Zero-base budgeting comes of age:
  what it is and what it takes to make it work.
  1977
  M Labor R 101:47-8 Ja '78. B. Burdetsky
Clarke, D. J. Irish blood
  Commonweal 105:120-2 F 17 '78. R. H. Balsam
Clark, E. Eyes, etc; a memoir
  New Leader 61:21-2 F 27 '78. A. Szogyi
Clarke, T. Last caravan
  Newsweek 91:76+ F 27 '78. M. Jefferson
Clissold, S. Wisdom of the Spanish mystics
  U.S. Cath 43:48-9 F '78. M. Christopher
Cohen, M. Sensible words: linguistic practice in
  England, 1640-1785
  Change 10:58-9 F '78. B. Yagoda
Cohen, M. N. Food crisis in prehistory: overpopu-
  lation and the origins of agriculture. 1977
  Science 199:676 F 10 '78. R. A. Diehl
Cornish, E. and others. Study of the future. 1977
  Phi Delta Kappan 59:426 F '78. H. Shane
Crew, L. ed. Gay academic
  Change 10:61 F '78
Crisp, Q. Naked civil servant
  America 138:128 F 18 '78. J. A. Tetlow

Davis, J. H. Guggenheims: an American epic
  N Y Times Bk R 83:10-11+ F 26 '78. F. Morton
Davis, S. H. Victims of the miracle: development
  and the Indians of Brazil
  Nation 226:181-3 F 18 '78. I. L. Horowitz
Davis, W. It's no sin to be rich: a defense of
  capitalism
  Nat R 30:223 F 17 '78. K. Mano
Dowley, T. ed. Eerdmans handbook to the his-
  tory of Christianity
  Chr Cent 95:137-9 F 1 '78. J. H. Smylie
Dubofsky, M. and Van Tine, W. R. John L.
  Lewis, A biography
  Progressive 42:40-1 F '78. W. Sinclair
Dumor, G. Stael
  Am Artist 42:81-2+ F '78. A. Werner

Eisler, B. ed. Lowell offering: writings by New
  England mill women (1840-1845)
  Nation 226:184-5 F 18 '78. E. Pochoda

Feinberg, G. What is the world made of? 1977
  Phys Today 31:53-4 F '78. R. A. Carrigan, jr
Fiedler, L. Freaks: myths and images of the
  secret self
  Newsweek 91:82-3 F 20 '78. W. Clemons
  Time 111:95-K11 F 20 '78. R. Z. Sheppard
Fields, R. M. Society under siege
  Commonweal 105:120-2 F 17 '78. R. H. Balsam
Fisher, L. and Lorie, J. H. Half century of re-
  turns on stocks and bonds. 1977
  Intellect 106:339-40 F '78. D. E. Farrar
Foster, D. W. and Foster, V. R. eds. Modern
  Latin American literature. 2v. 1975
  Américas 30:28 F '78. M. Gowland de Gallo
Foucault, M. Discipline and punish: the birth of
  the prison; tr. by A. Sheridan
  N Y Times Bk R 83:1+ F 19 '78. D. J. Roth-
  man
Fowlie, W. Journal of rehearsals: a memoir
  N Y Times Bk R 83:13+ F 19 '78. S. Gavron-
  sky
Franklin, H. B. Victim as criminal and artist:
  literature from the American prison
  N Y Times Bk R 83:14+ F 26 '78. A. Tracht-
  enberg
Fraser, M. Children in conflict
  Commonweal 105:120-2 F 17 '78. R. H. Balsam
French, R. M. Moon book. 1977

Figure 7-4. Selected book reviews from *Readers' Guide to Periodical Literature.*

Catholic Periodical and Literature Index, 1967 to date. Haverford, Pa.: Catholic Library Association, 1968—. Formerly Catholic Periodical Index 1930-1968.

>International in scope. Author and subject index to a selected list of Catholic periodicals. Cumulated at two-year intervals.

Humanities Index, 1974 to date. New York: H. W. Wilson, 1974—. Formerly International Index, 1907-1965, and Social Sciences and Humanities Index, 1965-1974.

>Indexes by author and subject articles in more than 250 periodicals in the humanities: archaeology, classical studies, folklore, history, language and literature, theology, and related subjects. In recent issues, book reviews are listed in a separate section in the back of the index under the authors of the books.

Social Sciences Index, 1974 to date. New York: H. W. Wilson, 1974—. Formerly International Index, 1907-1965, and Social Sciences and Humanities Index, 1965-1974.

>Gives author and subject entries for articles in more than 260 periodicals. Subjects covered include anthropology, area studies, economics, environmental science, geography, law and criminology, medical sciences, political science, psychology, public administration, sociology, and related subjects. Book reviews are in a separate section.

Subject

Agriculture

Biological and Agricultural Index, 1964 to date. New York: H. W. Wilson, 1964—. Formerly Agricultural Index, 1916-1964.

>A cumulative subject index to English language periodicals in the fields of biology, agriculture, and related sciences such as botany, food science, forestry, soil science, and veterinary medicine. A list of book reviews is located in the back.

Art

Art Index, 1929 to date. New York: H. W. Wilson, 1930—.

>Subject and author index to journals, museum bulletins, domestic art publications, and foreign journals. Subject areas included are: painting, sculpture, architecture, ceramics, graphic arts, landscape architecture, archaeology, and other related subjects.

Biography

Biography Index, 1946 to date. New York: H. W. Wilson, 1947—.

>Quarterly index to biographical material in books and about 1,900 different periodicals. Material is arranged: (1) by name of biographee and (2) by occupation or profession.

Business and Public Affairs

Business Periodicals Index, 1958 to date. New York: H. W. Wilson, 1958—. Formerly Industrial Arts Index, 1913-1957.

> Indexes magazines and journals in advertising, banking and finance, marketing, accounting, labor and management, insurance, and general business. Good source for information about an industry and about individual companies.

Public Affairs Information Service. Bulletin, 1915 to date. New York: Public Affairs Information Service, 1915—.

> Often called PAIS. Especially strong in public administration, political science, history, economics, finance, and sociology. Indexes books, pamphlets, society publications, and government documents as well as periodicals. Published twice monthly, cumulates annually.

Education

Education Index, 1929 to date. New York: H. W. Wilson, 1929—.

> A subject index to educational literature including periodicals, pamphlets, reports, and books. Subjects included: counseling and personnel service, teaching methods and curriculum, special education and rehabilitation, educational research, and many others covering all aspects of education. Monthly with annual cumulations.

Science and Technology

Applied Science and Technology Index, 1958 to date. New York: H. W. Wilson, 1958—. Formerly Industrial Arts Index, 1913-1957.

> Indexes by subject articles from scientific periodicals in the fields of aeronautics, automation, construction, electricity, engineering, and related subjects.

Engineering Index, 1884 to date. New York: Engineering Magazine, 1907-1919; American Society of Mechanical Engineers, 1920-1934; Engineering Index, Inc., 1934—.

> Reviews about 1,000 journals in engineering and related fields. Includes an abstract for each article cited. International in scope.

Abstracts

An *abstract* is an index which not only gives the location of the items cited but also includes a summary of the article or book. The abstracts are valuable as a reference source in that they index the scholarly literature from the academic and professional fields. The serious researcher, who is interested in finding out whether or not any research has been published on a particular topic, should consult the abstracts in that field. Many of the subject fields are covered by abstracting services. Some examples are: *Chemical Abstracts,* 1907 to date, which abstracts world literature related to chemistry appearing in books, reports, documents, and about 12,000 journals; *Sociological Abstracts,* 1952 to date, covering articles in all languages from journals concerned with sociology; and *Psychological Abstracts,*

1927 to date, containing summaries of journal articles, monographs, and reports on psychology and related studies. An excerpt from *Psychological Abstracts* is shown below.

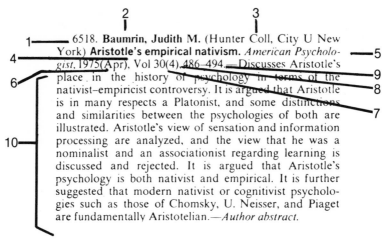

Figure 7-5.

1. Item number. Use as reference number in index section.
2. Author of article.
3. University with which author is affiliated.
4. Title of article.
5. Journal in which article appears.
6. Date of periodical.
7. Volume number.
8. Issue number.
9. Inclusive pages.
10. Summary of the article.

NEWSPAPER INDEXES

Newspaper indexes differ from periodical indexes in that they cover only one title. Periodical indexes give the library user references to many different publications, but the newspaper index gives access to the contents of only one newspaper. Usually newspaper indexes have only subject entries. As a rule the newspaper index does not give the exact title of an article which is often not too informative; instead, it gives a brief summary of the article. Newspapers are a good source for information on the local, state, national, and international levels. Most libraries subscribe to newspapers on a current and microfilm basis. The following titles are examples of widely used newspaper indexes:

New York Times Index, 1913 to date. New York: New York Times Co., 1913—. The Prior Series published by Bowker covers the years 1851-1912.

Subject index to The New York Times newspaper. Published twice monthly with annual cumulations. An excerpt from this index is shown below.

```
                              2
1—United States. See also subhead Intl Trade My 9
   3—Crop Controls and Subsidies. . . .
      4———Comment on Pres Ford's veto of farm price-support legis. which he main-
   tained would have been costly to taxpayers, consumers and consequently farmers
         6   7  89
   5—(S),My 4, IV, 2:1
```

Figure 7-6. Selected reference from *The New York Times Index,* May 1-15, 1975, page 3. "Copyright © 1975 by The New York Times Company. Reprinted by permission."

1. Primary subject heading.
2. See also cross reference.
3. Subdivision under the primary subject heading.
4. Brief summary of the newspaper article.
5. Indicates that the article is short.
6. Date of article. Year is found on the cover of index.
7. Section 4. Indicates the part of the newspaper in which the article is located.
8. Page 2.
9. Column 1.

Index to the Christian Science Monitor International Daily Newspaper, 1960 to date. Boston: Christian Science Monitor, 1960—.

Title of articles listed under subject with day, month, section, page, and column noted.

The Times Index (London), 1790 to date. Reading, England: Newspaper Archive Development, 1957—. Earlier issues are indexed under various titles.

Author and subject index not only to the daily Times, but also to the Sunday Times, The Times Literary Supplement, the Times Educational Supplement, and the Times Higher Education Supplement.

Wall Street Journal Index, 1958 to date. New York: Dow Jones, 1959—.

An index to a newspaper which emphasizes financial news.

The Washington Post Newspaper Index, 1972 to date. Wooster, Ohio: Bell and Howell, 1972—.

> Useful for coverage of news from the nation's capital. Originally part of the Newspaper Index, which also included the following newspapers: The Chicago Tribune, The Detroit News, The Houston Post, The Los Angeles Times, The New Orleans Times Picayune, and The San Francisco Chronicle.

INDEXES TO BOOK REVIEWS

Reviews of most new books and of forthcoming books are published in newspapers and magazines. Written by critics and journalists, book reviews provide descriptions and critical evaluations of books. The success or failure of a book's sale frequently depends on the kind of review it receives. Indexes to book reviews are good sources to locate references to reviews of books appearing in periodicals and newspapers. Some of these indexes have excerpts from the reviews, while others only list the sources. References to book reviews can also be located through periodical and newspaper indexes. Examples of some of the better-known indexes to book reviews are listed below.

Book Review Digest, 1905 to date. New York: H. W. Wilson, 1905—.

> This index is organized in two main sections. The first part is an alphabetical listing by authors of books. Each entry includes the title of the book, bibliographical information, and publisher's note. The publisher's note is followed by references to the reviews which appear in periodicals. Some of the references include excerpts from the book reviews. The second part is a subject and title index. A list of periodicals indexed is located in the front. Issued monthly with annual cumulation. See Figure 7-7.

Book Review Index, 1965 to date. Detroit: Gale Research, 1965—.

> Covers adult and juvenile fiction and non-fiction in the areas of humanities, social sciences, and library science. Reviews listed alphabetically by author of book. Beginning in 1976, a separate title index section included in the back of the book.

Current Book Review Citations, 1976 to date. New York: H. W. Wilson, 1977—.

> This is a cumulation of all reviews of books indexed in other Wilson indexes. Beginning in 1976, this index covers reviews published in more than 1,200 periodicals. Two separate parts: (1) author list which gives complete citation to reviews and (2) title listing which gives author's name. Periodicals indexed listed in the front.

Technical Book Review Index, 1917 to date. Pittsburgh: Carnegie Library, 1917-1929; New York: Special Libraries Association, 1935—.

> Topical arrangement of reviews which appear in scientific and technical journals. Entries give brief quotations from the reviews.

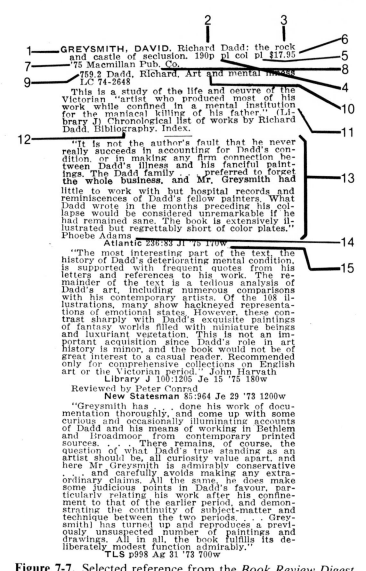

Figure 7-7. Selected reference from the *Book Review Digest.*

1. Author of book.
2. Title of book.
3. Sub-title of book.
4. Number of pages in the book.
5. Indicates book has plates and colored plates.
6. Price of book.
7. Year of publication.

8. Publisher.
9. Dewey Decimal number.
10. Main subject covered in the book.
11. Quotation from a review which appeared in *Library Journal.*
12. Describes auxiliary material found in the book.
13. Excerpt from a review which appeared in *Atlantic.*
14. Author of the review.
15. Excerpt is from a review which appeared in *Atlantic*, volume 236, page 83, July, 1975. The review has 170 words.

The following example is taken from the Subject and Title Index of *Book Review Digest*. It shows the subject entry for the book shown in Figure 7-7.

Art and mental illness
    Greysmith, D. Richard Dadd: the rock and castle of seclusion. (S '75)

INDEXES TO LITERATURE IN COLLECTIONS (ANTHOLOGIES)

Selected literary works of varied authorship have been placed together in one collection since the Greeks compiled the first *Greek Anthology* during the first and second centuries B.C. This first anthology is a collection of over 6,000 short poems and epigrams by some 320 authors. These works, considered the "flowers of literature," were given the name *anthology,* which means "a garland of flowers" or "gathered flowers." The practice of gathering the best work into a collection has resulted in much of the world's great literature being included in anthologies.

In modern times the term anthology refers to any collection of varied literary compositions. Works placed together in anthologies include poems, stories, essays, plays, and speeches. Anthologies can also include works from a period of history or works devoted to a particular subject or theme. Most anthologies include works of varied authorship, but it is not uncommon to have representative works of one author selected by an editor and collected in an anthology.

The outstanding characteristic of an anthology is the inclusion under one title of many different titles of shorter works. The titles of anthologies which a library owns, quite naturally, are listed in the card catalog. The titles of the shorter works found in the anthology, however, are not usually included in the card catalog. For example, the title, *Ten Modern Masters: An Anthology of the Short Story,* would be listed in the card catalog; the short story, "I'm a Fool," which is included in *Ten Modern Masters,* ordinarily would not be listed.

To analyze, or list, the contents of anthologies in the card catalog is costly and time-consuming. Instead, most libraries subscribe to various indexes which analyze the contents of literature in collections. Some of these indexes are described below.

Essays

Essay and General Literature Index, 1900 to date. New York: H.W. Wilson, 1900/1933—.

    An alphabetical author, subject, and sometimes title index to thousands of essays and chapters found in books. Particularly strong in the fields of the humanities and the social sciences. It is an excellent source for a criticism of an author's work.

SELECTED REFERENCES FROM *ESSAY AND GENERAL LITERATURE INDEX*

Consent (Law)
  Humphreys, L. G. The fallout of the legal mind in research. *In* Hook, S.; Kurtz, P. and Todorovich, M. eds. The ethics of teaching and scientific research p161-64

Conservation of natural resources
  Shaw, C. A. Dilemmas of supergrowth: depleting irreplaceable raw materials. *In* The Year book of world affairs, 1976 p273-91

  See also Human ecology

Conservatism
  Wolin, S. S. Hume and conservatism. *In* Livingston, D. W. and King, J. T. eds. Hume p239-56

Conservative Party (Great Britain)
  Arnold, M. The zenith of conservatism. *In* Arnold, M. The last word p122-43

Constitutional history. See Political science; and subdivision Constitutional history under names of countries, states, etc. e.g. United States—Constitutional history

Figure 7-8. Subject entry.

1. Subject heading.
2. Author of article.
3. Title of article.
4. Indicates article *in* the following work.
5. Editors of book.
6. Title of book.
7. Pages in book on which article appears.

Essay and General Literature Index. Copyright © 1977 by The H. W. Wilson Company. Material reproduced by permission of the publisher.

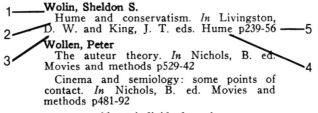

Wolin, Sheldon S.
  Hume and conservatism. *In* Livingston, D. W. and King, J. T. eds. Hume p239-56

Wollen, Peter
  The auteur theory. *In* Nichols, B. ed. Movies and methods p529-42
  Cinema and semiology: some points of contact. *In* Nichols, B. ed. Movies and methods p481-92

About individual works
  Signs and meaning in the cinema
  Abramson, R. Structure and meaning in the cinema. *In* Nichols, B. ed. Movies and methods p558-68

Figure 7-9. Author entry.

1. Author of article.
2. Title of article.
3. Editors of book.
4. Title of book.
5. Pages in book on which article appears.

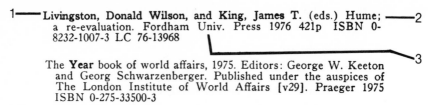

1——Livingston, Donald Wilson, and King, James T. (eds.) Hume; ——2
a re-evaluation. Fordham Univ. Press 1976 421p ISBN 0-
8232-1007-3 LC 76-13968

The Year book of world affairs, 1975. Editors: George W. Keeton
and Georg Schwarzenberger. Published under the auspices of
The London Institute of World Affairs [v29]. Praeger 1975
ISBN 0-275-33500-3

Figure 7-10. Selected references from List of Books Indexed.

1. Editors of book.
2. Title of book.
3. Publisher and date of publication.

Poetry

Granger, Edith. Granger's Index to Poetry. Ed. William James Smith. 6th ed., completely rev. and enl., indexing anthologies published through December 31, 1970. New York: Columbia University Press, 1973.

First published in 1904, this is considered the standard index to poetry. Each edition enlarges on the previous one, omitting some anthologies, adding new ones. Later editions arranged by sections as follows: (1) title and first-line index, (2) author index, and (3) subject index.

Plays

Connor, John M., and Billie M. Connor. Ottemiller's Index to Plays in Collections, an Author and Title Index to Plays Appearing in Collections Published between 1900 and Early 1975. 6th ed. Metuchen, N.J.: Scarecrow Press, 1976.

Index to full-length plays appearing in books published in England and the United States. It is divided into three sections: (1) author index with titles and dates of performance, (2) list of collections analyzed with key to symbols, and (3) title index.

Short Stories

Short Story Index, 1949 to date. New York: H. W. Wilson, 1953—. Supplements, 1950-1954, 1955-1958, 1959-1963, 1964-1968, 1969-1973, 1974, 1975. New York: H. W. Wilson, 1956-1975.

Supersedes Firkin's Index to Short Stories (1923) and its Supplements (1929-1936). First part is an author, title, and subject index. Second part is a list of collections indexed.

Speeches

Sutton, Roberta Briggs. Speech Index; an Index to 259 Collections of World Famous Orations and Speeches for Various Occasions. 4th ed., rev. and enl. New York: Scarecrow Press, 1966.

————, and Charity Mitchell. Supplement, 1966-1970. Metuchen, N.J.: Scarecrow Press, 1972.

Mitchell, Charity. Supplement, 1971-1975. Metuchen, N.J.: Scarecrow Press, 1977.

> Alphabetical arrangement of speeches by author, subject, and type of speech.

CRITICISM OF LITERARY WORKS

The following list of publications is useful in searching for commentaries, criticisms, interpretations, and explanatory information about literature of all kinds—novels, plays, poetry, and short stories. Some of the guides are limited to literature of a specific nationality, while others are international in their coverage. Both the titles and the annotations indicate in some measure the scope of the guide.

General

Essay and General Literature Index, 1900 to date. New York: H. W. Wilson, 1900/1933—.

> As noted earlier, this is an excellent source for criticism of all types of literature.

Novels

Adelman, Irving, and Rita Dworkin. The Contemporary Novel, a Checklist of Critical Literature on the British and American Novel since 1945. Metuchen, N.J.: Scarecrow Press, 1972.

> A selective survey of critical articles and essays of contemporary British and American novels in periodicals and books. Abbreviations used for periodicals listed in front before main entries and a bibliography of books analyzed is found in the back.

Gerstenberger, Donna, and George Hendrick. The American Novel, a Checklist of Twentieth Century Criticism. 2 vols. Denver: Allan Swallow, 1961-1970. Vol. 1, The American Novel 1789-1959. Vol. 2, Criticisms Written 1960-1968.

> Criticisms are listed under major authors by titles of works. Includes citations from books and periodicals.

Bell, Inglis Freeman, and Donald Baird. The English Novel 1578-1956: A Checklist of Twentieth-Century Criticisms. Denver: Allan Swallow, 1958.

> References to critical articles in books and periodicals. Arranged alphabetically by novelists and their individual works. Key to abbreviations of books and periodicals indexed included in the back.

Palmer, Helen H., and Anne Jane Dyson. English Novel Explication: Criticisms to 1972. Hamden, Conn.: Shoe String Press, 1973.

> Cites criticisms found in books and periodicals in English and foreign languages from 1958 to 1972.

Abernethy, Peter L., Christian J.W. Kloesel, and Jeffry R. Smitten. English Novel Explication. Supplement I. Hamden, Conn.: Shoe String Press, 1976.

> This work supplements and updates the Palmer and Dyson guide.

Kearney, E.I., and L.S. Fitzgerald. The Continental Novel, a Checklist of Criticism in English 1900-1966. Metuchen, N.J.: Scarecrow Press, 1968.

        Critical entries are organized under the following categories: the French novel, the Spanish and Portuguese novel, the Italian novel, the German novel, the Scandinavian novel, and the Russian and East European novel.

Plays

Breed, Paul F., and Florence M. Snideman. Dramatic Criticism Index; a Bibliography of Commentaries on Playwrights from Ibsen to the Avante-Garde. Detroit: Gale, 1972.

        Includes critical articles from over 200 periodicals and 630 books. Main entries under authors. Includes a title and a critic index.

Palmer, Helen H., and Anne Jane Dyson. American Drama Criticism Interpretations, 1890-1965, Inclusive of American Drama, since the First Play Produced in America. Hamden, Conn.: Shoe String Press, 1967. Supplement I, 1970. Supplement II, 1976. Comp. Floyd Eugene Eddleman.

        Lists critical articles of American plays located in periodicals, books, and monographs. Arrangement is alphabetical by playwright.

Palmer, Helen H. European Drama Criticism 1900-1975. Hamden, Conn.: Shoe String Press, 1977.

        A source book to critical writings of representative European plays in selected books and periodicals. Information is organized in three parts: (1) alphabetical list of playwrights with critical articles which appear in periodicals and books, (2) a list of books used as sources and a list of periodicals searched, and (3) an author-title index.

Poetry

Cline, Gloria Stark, and Jeffrey A. Baker. An Index to Criticisms of British and American Poetry. Metuchen, N.J.: Scarecrow Press, 1973.

        Cites critical articles on poetry published in periodicals and books between 1960 and 1970. List of abbreviations of periodicals used in entries and a bibliography of books cited are found in the back of this work.

Kuntz, Joseph M. Poetry Explication; a Checklist of Interpretation since 1925 of British and American Poems Past and Present. Rev. ed. Denver: Allan Swallow, 1962.

        Lists interpretations found in selected anthologies and periodicals.

Short Stories

Walker, Warren S. Twentieth-Century Short Story Explication; Interpretations 1900-1975 of Short Fiction since 1800. 3d ed. Hamden, Conn.: Shoe String Press, 1977.

        Analyses of short stories appearing in books, periodicals, and monographs.

SELECTED SUBJECT PERIODICAL INDEXES

Aerospace

Aerospace Medicine and Biology, 1964 to date. 1964—.
International Aerospace Abstracts, 1961 to date. 1961—.

Agriculture

Abstracts on Tropical Agriculture, 1975 to date. 1975—.
Animal Breeding Abstracts, 1933 to date. 1934—.
Bibliography of Agriculture, 1942 to date. 1942—.
Field Crop Abstracts, 1948 to date. 1948—.
Review of Applied Entomology, 1913 to date. 1913—.
Soils and Fertilizers, 1938 to date. 1938—.

Anthropology

Abstracts in Anthropology, 1970 to date. 1970—.

Aquatic Sciences

Aquatic Sciences and Fisheries Abstracts, 1971 to date. (Formerly *Aquatic Biology Abstracts,*
    1969-1971, and *Current Bibliography for Aquatic Sciences and Fisheries,* 1958-1971.)

Architecture

The Architectural Index, 1950 to date. 1950—.
Architectural Periodicals Index, 1972 to date. 1972—.

Art

Art and Archaeology Technical Abstracts, 1955 to date. 1955—.
Art in Life. 1965.
Art in Time. 1970.
Illustration Index (Greer), 1963-1971. 1973.
Index to Art Periodicals. 1962.
Index to Artistic Biography. 1973.

Astronomy

Astronomy and Astrophysics Abstracts, 1969 to date. 1969—.

Biology

Biological Abstracts, 1926 to date. 1926—.
Bioresearch Index, 1967 to date. 1967—. (Formerly *Bioresearch Titles,* nos. 1-12, 1965/66.)

Business

Accountants' Index, 1912 to date. 1921—.
Consumers Index to Product Evaluations and Information Sources, 1973 to date. 1973—.
F & S Index International: Industries, Countries, Companies, 1967 to date. 1967—.
F & S Index of Corporations and Industries, 1960 to date. 1960—.

Key to Economic Science and Managerial Sciences, 1976 to date. 1976—. (Formerly *Economic Abstracts,* 1953-1975.)

Personnel Management Abstracts, 1955 to date. 1955—.

Chemistry and Physics

Chemical Abstracts, 1907 to date. 1907—.

Electrical and Electronics Abstracts, 1966 to date. 1966—. (Formerly *Science Abstracts,* 1898—.)

Physics Abstracts, 1941 to date. 1941—. (Formerly *Science Abstracts,* 1898—.)

Criminology

Abstracts on Criminology and Penology, 1969 to date. 1969—. (Formerly *Excerpta Criminologica,* 1961-1968.)

Abstracts on Police Science, 1973 to date. 1973—.

Criminal Justice Abstracts, 1977 to date. 1977—. (Formerly *Crime and Delinquency Literature,* 1968-1977.)

Criminology Index, 1945-1972. 1975.

Ecology and Environment

Applied Ecology Abstracts, 1975 to date. 1975—.

Chicorel Index to Environment and Ecology, 1975 to date. 1975—.

Ecological Abstracts, 1974 to date. 1974—.

Environment Index, 1971 to date. 1971—.

MER (Man, Environment Reference) *Environmental Abstracts,* 1974 to date. 1974—.

Pollution Abstracts, 1970 to date. 1970—.

Selected Water Resources Abstracts, 1968 to date. 1968—.

Education

Business Education Index, 1940 to date. 1940—.

College Student Personnel Abstracts, 1965/66 to date. 1966—.

Current Index to Journals in Education (CIJE), 1969 to date. 1969—.

Exceptional Child Education Abstracts, 1969 to date. 1969—.

Energy

The Energy Index, 1973 to date. 1973—.

Energy Information Abstracts, 1976 to date. 1976—.

Renewable Energy Bulletin, 1974 to date. 1974—.

Ethnology

Abstracts of Popular Culture, 1977 to date. 1977—.

African Abstracts, 1950-1972. 1972.

Index to Literature on the American Indian, 1972 to date. 1972—.

Index to Periodical Articles by and about Blacks, 1960 to date. 1960—.

Food Science and Technology

Food Science and Technology Abstracts, 1969 to date. 1969—.
Nutrition Abstracts and Reviews, 1931/32 to date. 1932—.

Forestry

Forestry Abstracts, 1939/40 to date. 1940—.

Genetics

Genetics Abstracts, 1968/69 to date. 1969—.

Geography

Current Geographical Publications, 1938 to date. 1938—.
Geo Abstracts, 1972 to date. 1972—. (Formerly *Geographical Abstracts,* 1966-1971.)
A Guide to Geographic Periodicals. 1972.
A Tri-Index to Geography Periodicals. 1971.

Geology

Abstracts of North American Geology, 1966 to date. 1966—. (Formerly *GeoScience Abstracts,*
    1959-1966.)
Bibliography and Index of Geology, 1933 to date. 1934—.
Offshore Abstracts, 1974 to date. 1974—.
Petroleum Abstracts, 1961 to date. 1961—.

Health, Physical Education, and Recreation

Abstracts on Hygiene, 1926 to date. 1926—.
HPESR Abstracts, 1966/67 to date. 1967—.
Index and Abstracts of Foreign Physical Education Literature, 1955-1957. 1975.

History

America: History and Life, 1964 to date. 1964—.
Historical Abstracts: Parts A and B. 1955 to date. 1955—.
Writings on American History, 1902 to date. 1904—.

Horticulture

Horticultural Abstracts, 1931 to date. 1931—.

Human Resources

Human Resources Abstracts, 1973 to date. 1973—. (Formerly *Poverty and Human Resources
    Abstracts,* 1965-1972. 1972.)

Language and Literature

Abstracts of English Studies, 1958 to date. 1958—.
American Literature Abstracts, 1967, 1968-1972.
MLA Abstracts of Articles in Scholarly Journals, 1971 to date. 1971—.

Latin America

Index to Latin American Periodical Literature, 1929-1960. 8 vols. 1962. First Supplement, 1961-1965. 2 vols. 1968.
Index to Latin American Periodicals, 1961-1970. 1972.

Law

Index to Legal Periodicals, 1908 to date. 1908—.
Index to Periodical Articles Related to Law, 1958 to date. 1958—.

Library Science

Information Science Abstracts, 1969 to date. 1969—. (Formerly *Documentation Abstracts,* 1966-1969.)
Library Literature, 1921/32 to date. 1934—.

Mathematics

Mathematical Reviews, 1940 to date. 1940—.

Medicine

Allergy Abstracts, 1937 to date. 1937—.
Birth Defects, Abstracts of Selected Articles, 1964 to date. 1964—.
Dental Abstracts, 1956 to date. 1956—.
Index Medicus, 1960 to date. 1960—.
International Abstracts of Biological Sciences, 1956 to date. 1956—. (Formerly *British Abstracts of Medical Science,* 1954-1955.
Mental Retardation and Developmental Disability Abstracts, 1974 to date. 1974—. (Formerly *Mental Retardation Abstracts,* 1964-1973.)

Medieval Studies

International Guide to Medieval Studies, 1961 to date. 1961—.

Meteorology

Meteorological and Geoastrophysical Abstracts, 1950 to date. 1950—.

Microbiology

Microbiology Abstracts, 1965 to date. 1965—.

Military Science

Air University Library Index to Military Periodicals, 1949 to date. 1949—.

Music

Guide to the Musical Arts, 1953-1956. 1957.
Music Article Guide, 1966 to date. 1966—.
The Music Index, 1949 to date. 1949—.
Popular Music Periodicals Index, 1973 to date. 1974—.

Mycology

Abstracts of Mycology, 1967 to date. 1967—.

Nursing

International Nursing Index, 1966 to date. 1966—.
Nursing and Allied Health, 1977 to date. 1977—. (Formerly *Cumulative Index to Nursing and Allied Health Literature, 1956-1976.*)
Nursing Studies Index, 1970 to date. 1970—.

Oceanography

Oceanic Abstracts, 1966 to date. 1966—.
Oceanographic Index, 1946-1971. 1971-1976.

Philosophy

Philosopher's Index, 1967 to date. 1967—.

Political Science

ABC Pol Sci, 1969 to date. 1969—.
International Political Science Abstracts, 1951 to date. 1951—.

Population

Population Index, 1935 to date. 1935—.

Psychology

Psychological Abstracts, 1927 to date. 1927—.

Religion

Christian Periodical Index, 1958 to date. 1958—.
Guide to Social Science and Religion in Periodical Literature, 1964 to date. 1964—.
Religion Index One: Periodicals. 1978 to date. 1978—. (Formerly *Index to Religious Periodical Literature, 1949-1977.*)
Religious and Theological Abstracts, 1958 to date. 1958—.

Science

Applied Mechanics Reviews, 1948 to date. 1948—.
Computer Abstracts, 1957 to date. 1957—.
Metals Abstracts Index. 1968 to date. 1968—.
Nuclear Science Abstracts, 1948 to date. 1948—.
Science Citation Index, 1961 to date. 1961—.

Social Science

Social Sciences Citation Index, 1972 to date. 1973—.

Sociology

Sociological Abstracts, 1952 to date. 1952—.

Speech

DSH Abstracts, 1960 to date. 1960—.
Index to Journals in Communication Studies through 1974, 1975 to date. 1975—.
Speech Abstracts, 1970 to date. 1971—.
Speech Communication Abstracts, 1975 to date. 1975—.

Statistics

American Statistics Index, 1973 to date. 1973—.

Textiles

World Textile Abstracts, 1969 to date. 1969—.

Theater

Cumulated Dramatic Index, 1909-1949. 1965.
Guide to Dance Periodicals, 1931-1962. 1948-1963.
Guide to the Performing Arts, 1957 to date. 1960—.
The New York Times Theater Reviews, 1920-1970. 1971.
Theater/Drama Abstracts, 1974 to date. 1974—.

Traffic

Guide to Safety Literature, 1958 to date. 1958—.

Urban Affairs

Urban Affairs Abstracts, 1971 to date. 1971—.

Virology

Virology Abstracts, 1967 to date. 1967—.

Vocational Education

T & D Abstracts, 1975 to date. 1975—. (Formerly *CIRF Abstracts,* 1961-1974.)

Women

Women Studies Abstracts, 1972 to date. 1972—.

Zoology

Wildlife Review, 1952 to date. 1952—.
Zoological Record, 1864 to date. 1864—.

GOVERNMENT PUBLICATIONS

UNITED STATES GOVERNMENT PUBLICATIONS

The United States government is the largest publisher in the world. It publishes leaflets, pamphlets, periodicals, and books ranging in subject matter from Alabama agriculture to military information on Zaire. Thousands of publications pertain to a variety of subjects such as anthropology, business, defense, education, foreign relations, ecology, and medicine. Government publications come in all sizes and shapes from one page leaflets to works of several thousand pages and many volumes. Some are free or cost very little, while others cost as much as several hundred dollars.

The government issues many useful reference books such as the *Yearbook of Agriculture, Congressional Directory, Nautical Almanac, Statistical Abstract, Arctic Bibliography, Area Handbook(s)* for the countries of the world, *Pocket Guide(s)* to foreign countries, plus hundreds of others. Government documents give firsthand accounts of the exploration and settlement of America. Both the *Journals of the Continental Congress* and the *Journals of the Confederate States* are part of the United States government documents collection. Multivolume reports of the history of the United States' involvement in foreign wars are also available. The *Congressional Record* provides a verbatim account of the daily activities of Congress.

Each agency of the government specializes in certain fields of research, and the results of the research are printed by the Government Printing Office (GPO). The GPO is under the supervision of the Public Printer, who is chosen by the President with Senate approval. One of the most important officers in the GPO is the Superintendent of Documents, who is in charge of distribution of documents.

Individuals and groups can acquire documents by purchasing them or by borrowing them from depository libraries. Regional Depository Libraries, located in key places throughout the country, receive all unclassified publications of the GPO. Classified material is not distributed to the public, either because it has been reserved for "official use" or because its release allegedly would endanger the national security.

Libraries which serve as depository libraries usually establish separate documents collections which are kept in a separate area and which are not listed in the library's card catalog. Instead, the documents are checked in on shelf list cards and arranged according to the Superintendent of Documents' call number, called the SUDOCS number. Government documents, therefore, do not require the preparation of catalog cards and do not have card pockets like other library materials. Because government documents are usually shelved within a few days of their arrival, they are among the most current sources of information in the library.

Depository collections are shelved in the library according to the Superintendent of Documents Classification System (SUDOCS) which groups publications by government author—the agencies, bureaus, departments, or offices—as follows:

A	Agriculture
C	Commerce
D	Defense
HE	Health, Education, and Welfare
I	Interior
J	Justice
L	Labor
LC	Library of Congress
Pr	President's Office
S	State Department
SI	Smithsonian Institution
T	Treasury
TD	Transportation
VA	Veterans Administration
Y3.	Boards, Commissions and Committees Established by Act of Congress
Y4.	Agency Symbol of Congressional Committees

Publications are then organized and classified by the type of publication:

1:	Annual reports	5:	Laws
2:	General publications	6:	Regulations
3:	Bulletins	7:	Releases
4:	Circulars	8:	Handbooks, manuals, guides

The publications of the sub-agencies are assigned the main letters of the agency plus designated numbers for sub-agency. Publications of the Health, Education, and Welfare Department, for instance, use the abbreviation HE. The Social Security Administration publications are under HE 3; the Education Office, under HE 5; Social and Rehabilitation Service, under HE 17; Public Health Service, under HE 20; and Children's Bureau, under HE 21. The annual report for 1978 of the Secretary of Health, Education, and Welfare has the number HE 1.1:1978.

House and Senate documents and reports have been assigned serial numbers for almost two hundred years since *The American State Papers* were given the numbers 01 through 038. Congressional hearings, on the other hand, are found in the Y4. section of depository libraries. Publications of the Committee on Agriculture of the House are assigned the number Y4. Ag 8/1:; those of the Committee on Agriculture and Forestry of the Senate have the number Y4. Ag 8/2:.

To locate government publications which are handled separately and shelved by the SUDOCS call number, one must consult an index other than the card catalog. The Government Printing Office publishes the *Monthly Catalog of United States Government Publications,* (1895 to date), which serves as the major index to government publications. It is issued each month, and has annual, decennial, and quinquennial indexes. The publications are arranged alphabetically by issuing agency in the main body of the catalog. Each issue contains a subject, a title, and an author index. The following example is from the *Monthly Catalog's* subject index found at the end of the catalog.

1 _____ Plant-lice—Control

2 _____ Aphids on leafy vegetables: how to control them/,

        76-1435 _____ 3

Figure 8-1. Subject index.

Explanation:

1. Subject heading.
2. Title of document.
3. Entry number (refers to location of entry in the main body of the catalog).

Government publications listed in the *Monthly Catalog* since 1976 are described in much the same manner as material is described on a catalog card. Figure 8-2 shows the main entry for the document on Plant-lice Control listed above.

To find the publication described in Figure 8-2, one would proceed as follows:

1. Look in the subject index section under the heading "Plant-lice—Control."
2. Locate the entry number (76-1435) in the main entry section of the catalog.
3. Copy all pertinent information: author, title, issuing agency, date, and call number.
4. Locate the document by its SUDOCS call number on the depository library shelf.

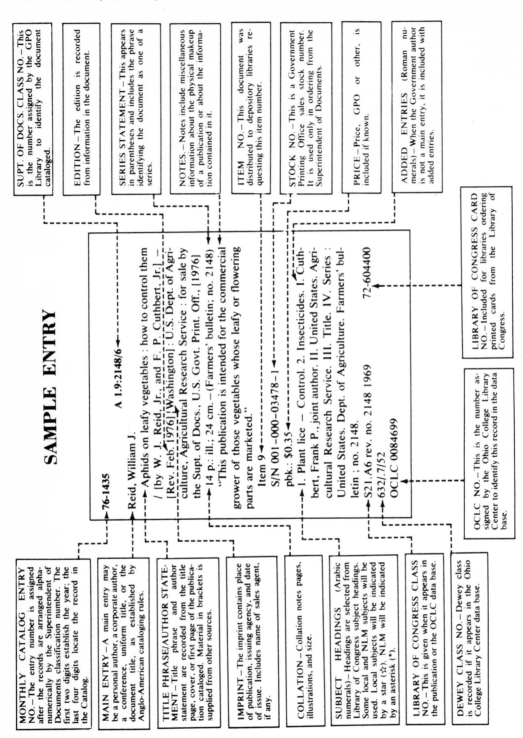

Figure 8-2. Monthly catalog of United States Government Publications.

Prior to 1976 items listed in the *Monthly Catalog* were arranged alphabetically by the name of the agency or branch of government responsible for its issuance. The following example is from a *Monthly Catalog* published prior to 1976:

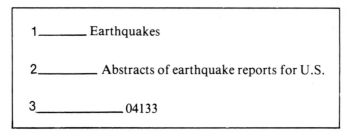

Figure 8-3. Subject index.

Explanation:

1. Subject heading.
2. Title of document.
3. Entry number.

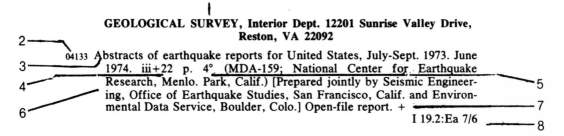

Figure 8-4. Main entry section of the catalog.

Explanation:

1. Issuing agency.
2. Entry number.
3. Title.
4. Pagination (3 preliminary pages + 22 pages of text).
5. Code number describing its size.
6. Imprint.
7. + indicates that the item is distributed by the issuing agency.
8. Superintendent of Documents call number or SUDOCS number.

The library user can eliminate much searching for materials listed prior to 1971 in the *Monthly Catalog* by using the *Cumulative Subject Index to the Monthly Catalog of U.S. Government Publications 1900-1971,* compiled by William Buchanan and Edna M. Kanely. This publication cites the document under the subject, then gives the year and page (or entry number) of the *Monthly Catalog* in which it is found. Figure 8-5 shows a page from the index.

LOUISIANA

See Also the names of cities, counties, companies,
and organizations located in Louisiana

Louisiana (07) 240; (08) 351; (09) 323; (10) 706
  abandoned customs boarding stations (16) 625
  aged and aging, problems, back-ground studies (61) 4120
  agricultural conservation handbook (40) 7; (51) 4062; (52)
    4360, 18095; (54) 1588; (55) 968, 18658; (57) 1328; (58)
    2732
  agricultural conservation program (41) 116, 1558; (43) 812;
    (44) 485; (45) 562; (46) 151; (47) 16; (49) 3702; (50) 6061
  Agricultural Experiment Station (10) 112, 234; (12) 141;
    (13) 331; (22) 495; (32) 1052; (37) 15; (40) 1016
  corn productiveness and mosaic disease (28) 209
  cotton, grade and staple length 1928-34 (36) 1291
  Livingston Parish soil survey (36) 519
  New Orleans, La. (18) 235
  rice (23) 383
  rice production experiments (26) 196
  steer feeding in sugar-cane belt (25) 733; (29) 909
  straighthead of rice (21) 627; (28) 146
  Webster Parish soil survey (16) 483
  agricultural loans (41) 947, 1560; (43) 262
  Agricultural Stabalization and Conservation Service, annual
    report (69) 8953
  agriculture (02) 483; (12) 460; (13) 334; (14) 184
  airports and seaplane bases, directory (40) 22
  alluvial soil in sugarcane area, deep-tillage investigations
    (67)1672
  and adjacent States, floods of Apr.-May 1958 (64) 2430
  annual crop summary (60) 1414
  annual survey of manufactures, 1960, standard metropolitan
    statistical areas, and large industrial counties,
    statistics (62) 18775; for 1961 (63) 4570; for 1962 (64)
    6031
  annual vegetable summary (60) 1415
  anopheles quadrimaculatus (20) 111
  archives (15) 166
  area measurement report (67) 13357
  attorneys (12) 666
  Board of Education -
    Emmett Cochran vs. (31) 359
  boundaries (09) 309, 315

Louisiana - Continued
  bridges - continued
    Red River (29) 455, 476, 723; (35) 802
    Sabine River (29) 358, 442, 476; (32) 964, 980, 981,
      1071, 1104; (35) 378, 507, 628, 666, 765
    Starks (28) 818, 994, 1103
    Sun (30) 1078
    Tensas River (27) 565
    See Also Atchafalaya River - Black River - Boeuf River -
      Chitto, Bogue - Ouachita River - Red River - Sabine
      River
  businessmen's organizations (44) 908
  Calcasien River and Pass -
    channel improvement, engineer report -
      departmental edition (61) 470
      document edition (61) 356
    salt water barrier system, construct, engineer report -
      departmental edition (63) 4838
      document edition (63) 4688
  campaign expenditures, 1932, U.S. Senate (33) 722
  cane sugar industry (18) 5, 17
  carrying mails, advertisements (34A) 325, 412
  case before Supreme Court (29) 328, 671
  case of Albert B. Fall (22) 675 .
  case of Secretary of Interior (25) 602
  cash farm income (60) 10492, 14805
  census of -
    agriculture, 1925 (21) 670; for 1920 (22) 70; tables
      5-8 (28) 80; for 1925 (29) 71; for 1930 (31) 1030; (32) 15,
      459; (33) 99, 171; 1935 (35) 1093; for 1935 (36) 1104;
      (37) 255; for 1940 (41) 623, 1715; (42) 167; 1945 (47) 360
    agriculture, 1950 -
      farm characteristics (52) 17405
      irrigation of agricultural land (53) 2083
    agriculture 1954, counties and State economic
      areas (56) 18505
    agriculture, 1959, counties (62) 4745
    agriculture, 1964, State and county statistics (67) 7509
    business 1948 -
      retail trade, statistics (51) 4593

William Buchanan and Edna M. Kanely, *Cumulative Subject Index to the Monthly Catalog of the United States Government Publications 1900-1971,* 15 vols. (Washington, D.C.: Carrollton Press, 1973), p. 837. Reproduced by permission of William Buchanan, publisher.

Figure 8-5.

The Congressional Information Service Index to Publications of the United States Congress (CIS, vol. 1-, no. 1-, Jan. 1970- Wash., 1970-), is a basic guide to Congressional actions. Part I provides brief abstracts to committee hearings, committee prints, House and Senate reports and documents, and miscellaneous publications of the U.S. Congress. Part II gives an in-depth index of subjects and names; an index of bills, reports, and documents; and an index of committee and subcommittee chairmen. It is published monthly with annual cumulations in two volumes (*CIS Annual*).

The *CIS/U.S. Serial Set Index* (Washington, D.C.: Congressional Information Service, 1975-) is a useful aid in locating Congressional publications—from the *American State Papers* in 1789 to 20th century publications. These indexes contain both finding lists and subject indexes.

One of the best sources for locating government statistics is the *American Statistics Index . . . A Comprehensive Guide and Index to the Statistical Publications of the U.S. Government,* 1973-(Washington, D.C.: Congressional Information Service, 1973-).

Government Periodicals

There are several ways to locate titles of United States government periodicals. Prior to 1976, the February issue of the *Monthly Catalog* listed government periodicals alphabetically by title. Since 1976 periodicals are listed in *The Monthly Catalog of United States Government Publications, Serial Supplement,* 1976-. John L. Andriot's *Guide to U.S. Government Serials and Periodicals,* 1959-1972 (McLean, Va.: Documents Index, 1959-1972), is a list of serials published by the United States Government.

To find information in government periodicals, the library user can consult the *Index to U.S. Government Periodicals, A Computer-Generated Guide to 156 Selected Titles by Author and Subject* (Chicago: Infordata International, 1970-).

Some periodical indexes listed in this text also index government periodicals.

Retrospective Indexes

Some useful indexes available to find the older publications of the Congress and other governmental agencies are listed as follows:

Poore, Ben Perley. *A Descriptive Catalogue of the Government Publications of the United States, September 5, 1775-March 4, 1881.* Washington, D.C.: Govt. Print. Off., 1885. (48th Cong. 2d sess. Misc. S. doc. 67)

Ames, John Griffith. *Comprehensive Index to the Publications of the United States Government, 1881-1893.* 2d ed. Washington, D.C.: Govt. Print. Off., 1905. (58th Cong. 2d sess. H. doc. 754)

Greely, Adolphus Washington. *Public Documents of the First to the Fourteenth Congress, Supplemented by a List of All Official Journals, Documents, and Reports of the First Fourteen Congresses 1789-1817, Papers Relating to Early Congressional Documents.* Washington: Govt. Print. Off., 1900. (56th Cong. 1st sess. S. doc. 428)

Documents Office. *Tables of and Annotated Index to the Congressional Series of United States Public Documents.* Washington, D.C.: Govt. Print. Off., 1902.

————. *Checklist of United States Public Documents 1789-1909. Congressional: to Close of 60th Congress. Departmental: to Close of Calendar Year 1909.* Vol. 1. *List of Congressional and Departmental Publications.* 3d ed. rev. and enl. Washington, D.C.: Govt. Print. Off., 1911.

————. *Catalog of the Public Documents of the 53d to 76th Congress and All Departments of the Government of the United States for the Period from March 4, 1893 to Dec. 31, 1940.* 25 vols. Washington, D.C.: Govt. Print. Off., 1896-1945.

————. *Index to the Reports and Documents of the 54th Congress., 1st Session to 72d Congress, 2d Session, December 2, 1895-March 4, 1933, with Numerical Lists and Schedule of Volumes.* 43 vols. Washington, D.C.: Govt. Print. Off., 1897-1933.

————. *Numerical Lists and Schedule of Volumes of the Reports and Documents of the 73d Congress—to date.* Washington, D.C.: Govt. Print. Off., 1934-.

GUIDES TO GOVERNMENT PUBLICATIONS

Morehead, Joe. *Introduction to United States Public Documents.* Library Science Text Series. Littleton, Colo.: Libraries Unlimited, 1975.

Schmeckebier, Laurence F., and Roy B. Eastin. *Government Publications and Their Use.* 2d rev. ed. Washington, D.C.: The Brookings Institution, 1969.

UNITED NATIONS PUBLICATIONS

The United Nations publishes documents of international interest. These publications may or may not be listed in the main card catalog along with the other resources of a library. In either case they may be shelved in a separate collection. The United Nations publishes several indexes which serve as guides to its publications. The *United Nations Documents Index* (1950-1970) is an index to publications of the General Assembly and the other principal organs of the United Nations. In 1970, the *United Nations Index* was superseded by three separate *UNDEX* indexes (*Subject Index, Country Index,* and *List of Documents Index*) which are published once a month except July and August. These indexes are in four languages (English, French, Russian, and Spanish).

The following books provide insight into the workings of the United Nations and its publications:

Everyman's United Nations; A Ready Reference to the Structure, Functions, and Work of the United Nations and Its Related Agencies. . . . Ed. 1-. New York: United Nations, Dept. of Public Information, 1948—.

McConaughy, John B., and Hazel Janet Blanks. *Students' Guide to United Nations Documents and Their Use.* New York: UN Council on International Relations and UN Affairs, 1969.

Stevens, Robert D., and Helen C. Stevens. *Reader in Documents of International Organizations.* Washington, D.C.: Microcard Editions Books, 1973.

Winton, Harry N.M., comp. *Publications of the United Nations System: A Reference Guide.* New York: Bowker, 1972.

BIBLIOGRAPHIC CITATIONS FOR UNITED STATES GOVERNMENT PUBLICATIONS

Government publications vary greatly according to type and form. Consequently, citations for government publications present many problems. The entries in the *Monthly Catalog of United States Government Publications* can serve as a guide for bibliographic citations, especially those since 1976 which are listed as they would be in the card catalog. The following general rules and examples should be helpful:

I. *Author*

    A. In citing documents indicate the name of the country first, unless the agency begins with *National* or *Federal.* For example:

        U.S. Office of Education
        National Aeronautics and Space Administration
        Federal Bureau of Investigation

    B. The agency of government as author.

        Bureaus and *offices* are entered as sub-headings *under the country,* not as sub-headings to the department unless the name of the bureau or office is not distinctive.

        U.S. Geological Survey *not* U.S. Interior Dept. Geological Survey.
        U.S. Geological Survey. Abstracts of North American Geology. Washington, D.C.: GPO, 1970.

    C. Divisions and sub-branches which are subordinate to executive departments, ministries, bureaus, and the like are entered as subheadings to those departments, ministries, bureaus, etc.

        U.S. Library of Congress. General Reference and Bibliography Division. Children's Literature, a Guide to Reference Sources. Comp. Virginia Haviland. Washington, D.C.: GPO, 1966.

    D. Personal authors can be used for nonadministrative publications, reports not by an official, parts of a series, single addresses, and collected editions, as well as collections of treaties of several countries compiled by an individual. The name of the issuing agency and other identifying information should be placed in parenthesis following the imprint.

        Reid, William J., Jr., and F.P. Cuthbert, Jr. Aphids on Leafy Vegetables: How to Control Them. Washington, D.C.: GPO, 1976. (Dept. of Agriculture, Agricultural Research Service, Farmers' Bulletin no. 2148).

If the individual author is known but the agency is listed first, the individual's name is placed after the title and is preceded by a comma and the word "by."

> U.S. Consumer Product Safety Commission. <u>Hazard Analysis of Aluminum Wiring,</u> by Rae Newman. Washington, D.C.: GPO, 1975.

II. *Titles.* The title of the publication follows the author's name and should be *underlined.* In citing a Congressional document, include such information as the number and session of Congress and the type and number of publication. This should not be underlined.

III. *Imprint.* Most U.S. government publications are published by the Government Printing Office regardless of the agency which issues it. The imprint for publications of the Government Printing Office is:

> Washington, D.C.: GPO, date. (See preceding examples.)

Since the GPO is not always the publisher, sometimes it will be necessary to use the imprint listed in the *Monthly Catalog* in the citation.

> U.S. Energy Research and Development Administration. <u>Development of a Modular Software System for Dynamic Simulation of Coal Conversion Plants.</u> Springfield, Va.: National Technical Information Service, 1976.

IV. *Types of publications*

A. Laws, decrees

> U.S. Laws, Statutes, etc. <u>Clean Water Act of 1977.</u> Approved Dec. 27, 1977. P.L. 217, 95 Cong., 1st sess. Washington, D.C.: GPO, 1977. (91 Stat. 1566)

B. Congressional hearings

> U.S. Cong. Senate. Select Committee on Nutrition and Human Needs. <u>Federally Supported Food Programs:</u> . . . . 95th Cong., 1st sess. Washington, D.C.: GPO, 1977.

> U.S. Cong. House. Committee on Banking, Finance and Urban Affairs. <u>Conduct of Monetary Policy, Pursuant to the Full Employment and Balanced Growth Act of 1978,</u> P.L. 95–523. 96th Cong., 1st sess. Washington, D.C.: GPO, 1979.

C. Bills and Reports

> U.S. Cong. Senate. Committee on Finance. <u>Title V of the Deep Seabed Mineral Resources Act.</u> Report to accompany S. 493, 96th Cong., 1st sess. Washington, D.C.: GPO, 1979.

> U.S. Cong. House. Committee on the Judiciary. <u>Opposing the Granting of Permanent Residence in the United States to Certain Aliens.</u> Report to accompany H. Res. 795. 95th Cong., 1st sess., H.R. no. 691. Washington, D.C.: GPO, 1977.

D. Document

> U.S. Cong. House. <u>Federal Election Campaign Laws Relating to U.S. House of Representatives.</u> 94th Cong. 1st sess., House Doc. 190. Washington, D.C.: GPO, 1975.

> U.S. Cong. Senate. <u>Scarce World Resources Debate Topic, 1975–76.</u> 94th Cong. 1st sess., Senate Doc. no. 45, Serial 13105–1. Washington, D.C.: GPO, 1975.

E. Court Case

   Brewer v. Williams. 430 U.S. 389 (1977).
   (Interpretation: Name of case, volume 430, U.S. Reports, page 389, date 1977)

F. *Congressional Record*

   Cong. Rec., 10 April 1975, pp. 5823–5824.
   Notice that it is not necessary to cite the subject or title of the article or its author.

V. *Abbreviations:*

Cong.—Congress
HR—House of Representatives
HR 190—House bill
S—Senate
S 45—Senate bill
H. Res—House resolution
S. Res—Senate resolution
H. Rept.—House report
S. Rept.—Senate report
H. Doc.—House document
S. Doc—Senate document
Cong. Rec.—Congressional Record
GPO—Government Printing Office

Imprint   place of publication, publisher, and either publication or copyright date.

Index   alphabetical list of the subjects discussed in the book with corresponding page number; also separate publication which points to information found in other sources.

Introduction   describes the subject matter and gives a preliminary statement leading to the main contents of the book.

Italic   kind of type in which the letters usually slope to the right and which is used for emphasis.

Journal   scholarly periodical usually issued monthly or quarterly.

Preface   gives the author's purpose in writing the book and acknowledges those persons who have helped in its preparation.

Reprint   copies of the same edition printed at a later time.

Scope   the range of material covered in a book or article.

Serial   publications issued on a continuing basis at regularly stated intervals.

Series   publications similar in content and format.

Short-title   first part of a compound title.

Stacks   groups of shelves on which books are placed in a library.

Sub-title   second half of a compound title which explains the short-title.

Table of Contents   a list of chapters or parts of a book in numerical order with the pages on which they are located.

Title page   page in front of the book which gives the official author, title, and often the imprint.

Vertical file   files containing ephemeral materials such as pamphlets, pictures, and newspaper clippings, which are not listed in the card catalog.

Volume   written or printed sheets put together to form a book. One book of a series. All the issues of a periodical bound together to make a unit.

Glossary

Abstract   a type of index which gives the location of an article in a periodical or a book and a brief summary of that article.

Annotation   critical or explanatory note about the contents of a book or an article.

Appendix   section of the book containing supplementary materials such as tables or maps.

Article   a complete piece of writing that is part of a larger work.

Bibliography   list of sources of information.

Blurb   advertisement found on the book jacket designed to promote the sale of the book.

Book number   last letter/number combination in the call number. Stands for the author of the book and sometimes the title.

Call number   the identification number which determines where a book or other library material is located in the library.

Class number   top part of call number which stands for subject matter of the book.

Colophon   a publisher's emblem, also inscription at the end of the book describing the type of print, the paper, and other facts concerning its production.

Copyright   the legal right to control the production, use, and sale of copies of a literary, musical, or artistic work.

Contemporary   happening or existing at the same time.

Cross reference   a reference from one term or word in a book or index to another word or term.

Cumulation   an index which is formed as a result of the incorporation of successive parts of elements. All the material is arranged in one alphabet.

Current   existing at the present time.

Edition   all copies of a book printed from a single type setting.

Footnotes   identification of reference sources used in a text, placed at the bottom of the page (or end of a chapter), also explanatory notes.

Frontispiece   illustration or portrait facing the title page of a book.

Glossary   a list with definitions of technical or unusual terms used in the text.

Imprint   place of publication, publisher, and either publication or copyright date.

Index   alphabetical list of the subjects discussed in the book with corresponding page number; also separate publication which points to information found in other sources.

Introduction   describes the subject matter and gives a preliminary statement leading to the main contents of the book.

Italic   kind of type in which the letters usually slope to the right and which is used for emphasis.

Journal   scholarly periodical usually issued monthly or quarterly.

Preface   gives the author's purpose in writing the book and acknowledges those persons who have helped in its preparation.

Reprint   copies of the same edition printed at a later time.

Scope   the range of material covered in a book or article.

Serial   publications issued on a continuing basis at regularly stated intervals.

Series   publications similar in content and format.

Short-title   first part of a compound title.

Stacks   groups of shelves on which books are placed in a library.

Sub-title   second half of a compound title which explains the short-title.

Table of Contents   a list of chapters or parts of a book in numerical order with the pages on which they are located.

Title page   page in front of the book which gives the official author, title, and often the imprint.

Vertical file   files containing ephemeral materials such as pamphlets, pictures, and newspaper clippings, which are not listed in the card catalog.

Volume   written or printed sheets put together to form a book. One book of a series. All the issues of a periodical bound together to make a unit.

Index

Note: Only reference books and indexes that are discussed in the text are listed in this index by title. For additional titles consult the lists at the end of Chapters 6, 7, and 8.